EQ6 PIECED DRAWING
Exercises in Pieced Block Design by Patti R. Anderson

COMPANION BOOK 3

The Electric Quilt Company
419 Gould Street, Suite 2
Bowling Green, Ohio 43402

EQ6 Pieced Drawing
Copyright © 2007
By Patti R. Anderson
All rights reserved.

The Electric Quilt Company
419 Gould Street, Suite 2
Bowling Green, OH 43402 USA

419/352-1134 (general)
800/356-4219 (sales only)
419/352-4332 (fax)
Find us online at: www.electricquilt.com

Any corrections and/or clarifications to sections of this book after it has been printed can be found online at: www.electricquilt.com > Support > Frequently Asked Questions > EQ6

No part of this book may be reproduced in any form except by the original purchaser for their own personal use. The written instructions and designs are intended for the personal use of the retail purchaser and are protected under copyright laws. They are not to be photocopied, duplicated or reproduced by any means for commercial use.

We do encourage the use of this book for teaching purposes. Teachers may use the information from the chapters of this book as lessons to teach EQ6 if they give credit to Patti R. Anderson and *EQ6 Pieced Drawing*. Copyright law forbids teachers from reproducing any part of the printed material for distribution to students. Students wanting a copy of the lesson will need to purchase the book.

CREDITS:
Book Editor: Sara Seuberling
Book and Cover Design: Sara Seuberling
Book Layout: Amy Hagan
Technical Reviewers: Andrea Bishop

Block designs shown on the front cover designed by Patti R. Anderson.

Acknowledgments

My sincerest thanks go to:

- **All the folks of the Electric Quilt Company.** Extra special thanks go to **Dean Neumann, Penny McMorris, Sara Seuberling, Ann Rutter, Andrea Bishop, and Amy Hagan** who all had a part in the content and polish of this book. Your talents, skills and hard work make me look good—thanks! I say it with utmost sincerity when I say what a very special bunch of people you are to work with.

- **Fran Gonzalez**, whose talent, insight, humor and stature are an inspiration to any EQ user.

- **Carol and Roger Miller** at Quilt University, whose organizational skills and business savvy have made EQ classes available worldwide. Teaching classes at QU has allowed me to encounter EQ users I might never have met before.

- **Members of Info-EQ mailing list and all my students at QuiltUniversity.com.** Your valued input, questions, and insatiable desire to learn more about EQ has inspired much of what is covered in this book. Keep up the good work!

- My sister, **Karen Vanoster.** It's so nice to have a quilting buddy in the family who understands what this is all about.

- My husband, **Robert M. Anderson**. Thanks for being my cheerleader through the late nights, missed dinners and long hours spent at the computer. I know I could not have written this book without you!

About the Author

Patti R. Anderson is a professional quiltmaker, quilt teacher and pattern designer from West Virginia. Along with regular quilt classes, she currently teaches beginner EQ classes around the state and intermediate and advanced EQ classes at QuiltUniversity.com.

Patti has become best known for her ability to push EQ's block drawing potential to the limits and beyond, and loves to share and teach that knowledge with others. Some of this shared knowledge you'll find on her website in her "EQ Patch" at www.patchpieces.com.

Patti has been sewing since she was nine years old and has been quiltmaking for over almost 20 years. She spent her first years as a quiltmaker selling her quilts and quilted products on consignment and in shops under the name Patchpieces. Patti no longer makes quilts to sell, but now concentrates her energies and talents to teaching others to quilt and to use EQ.

Patti lives in Spencer, West Virginia with her husband Robert Anderson, who is a United Methodist pastor. They have two lovely daughters both married now and starting families of their own. Left at home with Bob and Patti is their Husky-mutt dog, Grommit, who likes to make sure that she is the center of attention now that that her masters are empty-nesters.

Table of Contents

Introduction 7
Inches versus Centimeters 9
Using the Precision Bar 10
Adding Blocks to My Library 12

Chapters 15
Chapter 1: Click and Draw Blocks with
Pieced PatchDraw 17
Chapter 2: Basic Pieced Block Drawing 55
Back to the Drawing Board 56
Chapter 3: Divide & Conquer! 91
Chapter 4: Drawing Outside the Box 135

Index 205
Precision Bar Reference 211
Tools Quick Reference 213

EQ6 Pieced Drawing

EQ6 PIECED DRAWING
Exercises in Pieced Block Design by Patti R. Anderson

Introduction

Introduction

When I was in college (we won't say how long ago that was!) I took several years of French. I remember my French teacher telling the class over and over, "You must use it or you'll lose it." Unfortunately, I didn't heed her advice so I never learned to speak the language fluently. What does that have to do with EQ6 and drawing blocks? To really learn to draw blocks in EQ6 you must play with it often. This book is designed to help you do that! It will help you learn the "language" of EQ6 so that you can draw more fluently and be able to create blocks as if you spoke the language naturally.

About this book…

This book is all about drawing blocks. In particular it's about drawing pieced blocks. We'll be using only the EasyDraw™ worktable and the Pieced layer of the PatchDraw. I may throw in a suggestion for a quilt layout if I feel it is needed, but the purpose of this book is to teach you the skills to draw blocks using all the wonderful tools and features EQ6 provides for us—that is more than enough to fill a book! You may not even realize it (because you are having so much fun drawing blocks), but as you work through this book, you will have touched on nearly every drawing tool and feature that EasyDraw™ and the Pieced layer of PatchDraw have to offer. Pretty sneaky, eh?

As I mentioned earlier we are going to be working only on pieced blocks. I hesitate to say traditional pieced block, because a lot of what you will learn as you work through the exercises is meant to take you beyond the traditional. At your request, I have included more variations for you to try at the end of each exercise. The exercises are organized loosely in progressive order, but don't feel you have to start at the beginning. Choose an exercise that interests you and if you get stuck, refer back to earlier ones.

The exercises in this book assume that you have worked through the six lessons in the *EQ6 User Manual* and have watched most of the help videos. If you have done at least this, you should be somewhat familiar with the basics of EQ6. If you have not worked through these lessons in the manual, I highly encourage you to do so before proceeding with the exercises in this book. If you have worked through *EQ6 Simplified* by Fran Gonzalez, you will be even better prepared for the exercises in this book. In other words, you will have a lot more fun with this book if you are familiar with the basics of EQ6!

I will not instruct you to start a new project file with each exercise, but I recommend that you do so because many of the exercises will generate numerous blocks. Name your project file similar to the exercise and use the Notecard feature to identify blocks, so you can easily locate them later.

Have fun learning the language of drawing and may you create a library full of blocks to rival any quilt book!

Patti R. Anderson

Inches versus Centimeters...

The exercises in this book were written based on inches, but should work fine if you are using centimeters. I use graph paper divisions extensively so use these divisions as a guideline to visualize how you set up your drawing board to work with metric. You can change the Block worktable to use inches or centimeters. Click **FILE > Preferences**, and then under Workspace/Measurement choose the measurement unit you prefer. Please note that changing the measurement unit does NOT convert sizes. If a block is 12 inches and you switch to centimeters the block will be 12 centimeters.

As a general rule, set the snap to grid points to be a multiple of the block size and to match your ruler divisions whether using inches or centimeters.

If you are working in inches and your block is 6" x 6", you should set both your horizontal and vertical snap points to:

- 6 (snap every inch, 6 x 1 = 6)
- 12 (snap every 1/2 inch, 6 x 2 = 12)
- 24 (snap every 1/4 inch, 6 x 4 = 24)
- 48 (snap every 1/8 inch, 6 x 8 = 48), etc.

If you are working in centimeters and your block is 15 x 15cm, you should set both your horizontal and vertical snap points to:

- 15 (snap every cm, 15 x 1 = 15)
- 30 (snap every 0.5cm, 15 x 2 = 30)
- 75 (snap every 2mm, 15 x 5 = 75)
- 150 (snap every mm, 15 x 10 = 150), etc.

Introduction

Using the Precision Bar

The Precision Bar is a toolbar that sits just below the top menu bar. It gives you a quick and handy way to change things like block size or whether or not to display graph paper on your block. (The slower way would be to choose these items from the BLOCK menu > Drawing Board Setup.) The choices available on the Precision Bar change depending on which block style you're working on.

The Precision Bar is in my top FFF's (five favorite features) of EQ6. Those of you familiar with previous EQ versions will know how handy the Precision Bar is for quickly getting set to draw.

If you are new to EQ6, lucky you! I'm sure you'll learn to love the Precision Bar too, when you see how quickly it allows you to change drawing settings like block size, snap to grid points and graph paper size.

1. Click **WORKTABLE > Work on Block** on the top menu bar.

2. If the Precision Bar is not showing on the Block worktable, click **VIEW > Precision Bar** on the top menu bar. (If a check appears beside *Precision Bar*, then the Precision Bar is on the worktable already.)

Precision Bar

Step 1

Step 2

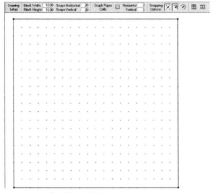

Worktable with Precision Bar

EQ6 Pieced Drawing

Introduction

Step 3

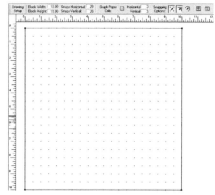

Worktable with Block Rulers

Step 4   on   on   off

Double-click to change numbers

Step 5

3. Click **VIEW > Block Rulers** on the top menu bar to make sure that the block rulers are showing.

4. As we begin drawing, unless the exercise instructs otherwise, make sure you have:

   - Snap to grid **ON**
   - Snap to Node **ON**
   - Snap to Drawing **OFF**

   These are the default settings, so it is very important to remember them.

5. When you are instructed to use the Precision Bar to change the block size, snap to grid points or graph paper divisions, here's how: **Double-click** inside the number box (to highlight the current number). Type your new number. Press your keyboard **ENTER** key to make the change to the drawing board. Or press your keyboard **TAB** key to move to the next box on the Precision Bar.

   On the EasyDraw™ Precision Bar, if you start by highlighting the Block Width box you can move your way to graph paper divisions and back again using the **TAB** key. I love this!

Companion Book Three   **11**

Introduction

Adding Blocks to My Library

Although I will not instruct you to save blocks to My Library in the exercises, you will definitely want to know how to do this. I recommend you add a custom library for each chapter, and then you can rename the styles to indicate the exercises.

Assuming that you will want to create a custom library for the exercises in this book here are some brief instructions on how you can do this. For more information about using My Library see pages 143-146 of the *EQ6 User Manual*.

Adding a Custom Block Library

1. Start a new project file or open an existing project file. You don't need to add any blocks to the Sketchbook in this first part; we're just going to create the categories to use later.

2. Click **LIBRARIES > Block Library**. Click on the blue **My Library** bar on the left to open that section.

3. Click the **Add Library** button at the bottom-left of the Block Library window.

4. Type the name *EQ6 Pieced Drawing Chapter 1*. Type in a number of styles. The default number of styles is 10. Change this to **6** for now. You can always modify it later.

5. Click **OK** to add the new category for Chapter 1.

6. *Repeat* the above to add a new library category for each chapter (there are four of them). For now, leave the number of styles at 10, you can modify these later as needed.

7. To rename a style, click on the Library you want to modify. Right-click on the style name and choose **Modify Style** from the context menu. Under your Chapter 1 category, choose Style 1 first and rename it *Pieced PatchDraw Rectangle* or something similar to indicate the exercise. Click **OK**. There are six exercises in Chapter 1, so you can rename each of the six styles accordingly (Pieced PatchDraw Rectangle, Pieced PatchDraw Circle, Pieced PatchDraw Arc, etc.).

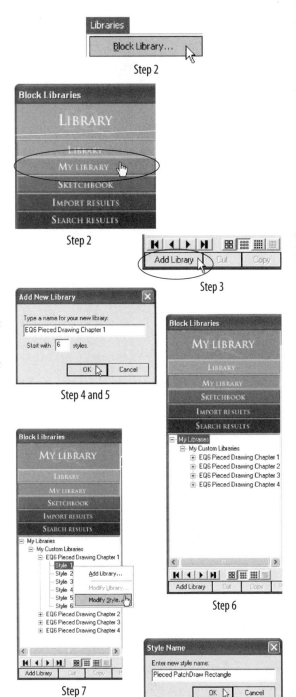

12   EQ6 Pieced Drawing

Introduction

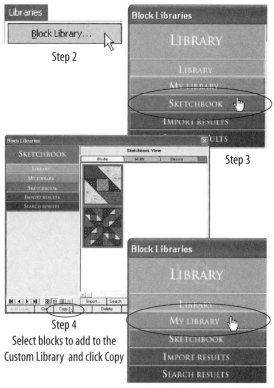

Step 2

Step 3

Step 4
Select blocks to add to the
Custom Library and click Copy

Step 5

Step 6

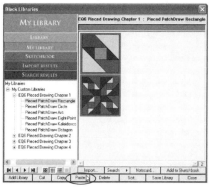

Step 7

Step 7

Step 7

Adding Blocks from the Sketchbook to your Custom Library

(Note: Work through the first exercise in Chapter 1 and then you'll have several blocks to add!)

1.   Open a project file from which you want to save blocks to your My Library.

2.   Click **LIBRARIES > Block Library**.

3.   Click on the blue **Sketchbook** bar on the left to open that section. If no blocks display, simply click the blue **Library** bar on the top-left and select a few blocks to **Add to Sketchbook** for this exercise. You can delete them later. Now, click the blue **Sketchbook** bar again.

4.   Click to select the blocks you want to add to My Library. Select multiple blocks one at a time by holding down the **CTRL** key. Holding down the **SHIFT** key will select all the blocks between any two that you select. **CTRL+A** will select all the blocks in the Sketchbook. When you have the blocks you want to add selected, click on the **Copy** button.

5.   Click on the blue **My Library** bar to open that section and then click on the category and style in which you want to add your blocks.

6.   Click on the **Paste** button to add the copied blocks. Your copied blocks should show in the My Library window after you paste them.

7.   When you're finished adding blocks, click on the **Save Library** button. Click **OK**, and then click **Close** to close the Block Library.

Some exercises will generate numerous blocks and some perhaps only a few. Glance over the exercise first and then use your own judgment as to how you want to rename the styles under each chapter category.

Whew! Now that the introductions are over, I think it's time to start drawing.

Companion Book Three   **13**

EQ6 PIECED DRAWING
Exercises in Pieced Block Design by Patti R. Anderson

Chapters

Click and Draw Blocks with Pieced PatchDraw

In this chapter we will cover a fun and fast way of drawing pieced blocks. New to EQ6 is the Pieced layer of PatchDraw (which I refer to as Pieced PatchDraw in this book). With Pieced PatchDraw, you build your block with closed patches. You can clone, flip, rotate, and move a patch or groups of patches to create an entire block very quickly. Once the block is completely filled with shapes, you can print foundation patterns and rotary cutting instructions just like for any other pieced block.

In Pieced PatchDraw if you can click a mouse button, you can draw a block! You don't need to know advanced math to create spectacular blocks—that part is done for you when using the special grids. Using one of the new Polydraw tools (PolyLine or PolyArc) you click around the special grids to create patches to fill the block. There are six special grids you can choose from: Rectangle, Circle, Arc, Eight Point Star, Kaleidoscope and Octagon.

If you have not done so already, read through the sections in the *EQ6 User Manual* just to get familiar with some of the terms of Pieced PatchDraw (pages 101-102 and pages 238-239). I will cover much of the same in this chapter, but much more in depth.

The exercises in this chapter will introduce you to each of the six special grids of Pieced PatchDraw. Along the way you will learn to use the tools and grids. I recommend working through the exercises in this chapter in the order they are presented, as I have added special tips and information throughout the first exercises that you will want to know before proceeding to the next.

At the end of each Pieced PatchDraw grid exercise you will find a special section called "Show & Draw." I will present you with 16 blocks to try on these special grids. Because drawing with Pieced PatchDraw is so easy, all you'll need is the Precision Bar settings for the block and then you can click your way to a Sketchbook full of new blocks. I am sure by the time you work your way through these blocks you will begin to think of a gazillion more blocks you can create with Pieced PatchDraw. Let's get started!

Important Tips for Pieced PatchDraw **18**

Pieced PatchDraw Rectangle **19**

Pieced PatchDraw Circle **25**

Pieced PatchDraw Arc **34**

Pieced PatchDraw Eight-Point Star **39**

Pieced PatchDraw Kaleidoscope **46**

Pieced PatchDraw Octagon **51**

Chapter 1

Important Tips for Pieced PatchDraw

- It does not matter where you begin drawing. Just remember to end the patch at the same point where you began.

- Press your keyboard **ESC** key or double-click on the worktable to remove the entire drawing while still in the drawing mode.

- Hold down your keyboard **SHIFT** key and click to detach the last anchored point from the grid—removing the last drawn segment while still in the drawing mode.

- Do not use **EDIT > Undo** while still in the drawing mode. It will undo your last action before you began drawing with the PolyLine or PolyArc tool. It will not undo your drawing while in the drawing mode. To undo while still in drawing mode, use the **ESC** key or **SHIFT** key as noted above.

- The Pieced layer of the PatchDraw worktable is permanently set to **Snap to Grid**. When you are using the PolyLine or PolyArc tools, you will notice the segments snapping to the closest grid point.

- Patches are automatically selected after you double-click to close them, allowing you to clone, rotate, and move your patch without switching to the Pick tool.

- To move a selected patch, position your cursor over the four-headed arrows in the center of the patch, click, hold and drag the patch to the new location.

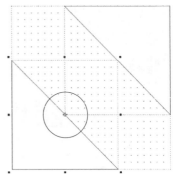

To move patches, position cursor over *center* of selected patch

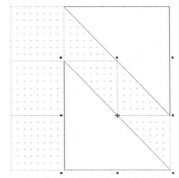

Click, hold and drag the patch to its new location

Chapter 1: Click and Draw Blocks with Pieced PatchDraw

Example of *Garret Windows* Block

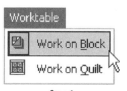

Step 1

Step 2

Step 3

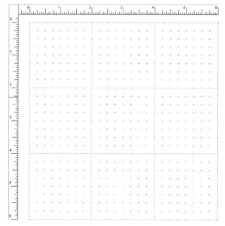

Rectangle Drawing Board

Polydraw Tools

Step 4
PolyLine

Pieced PatchDraw Rectangle

You can draw just about any rectangular block with this grid on the Pieced layer of PatchDraw. Let's begin by creating a simple *Garret Windows* block. You'll see how quickly you can build a block with closed shapes in Pieced PatchDraw.

1 Click **WORKTABLE > Work on Block** on the top menu bar.

2 Click **BLOCK > New Block > PatchDraw Block** on the top menu bar.

3 On the Precision Bar, enter these values pressing your keyboard TAB key after each:

- Block Width = **6.00**
- Block Height = **6.00**
- Grid: **Rectangle**
- Snaps Horizontal = **24**
- Snaps Vertical = **24**
- Graph Paper visibility is toggled **ON**
- Cells Horizontal = **3**
- Cells Vertical = **3**

Can you see the grid dots? EQ6 lets you choose large or small grid dots. You will probably find large dots make it much easier to draw the patches. To change the dot size, click **BLOCK > Drawing Board Setup > Snap Grid**. Under Grid Display, click *Display large grid dots*. You can also change grid dot color if you like. Click **OK**.

4 **Click and hold** on the **Polydraw** tool to make the PolyLine and PolyArc tools appear on the flyout. Click the **PolyLine** tool.

Companion Book Three **19**

Chapter 1: Click and Draw Blocks with Pieced PatchDraw

We're going to draw two half-square triangles—one in the upper-right corner; one in the lower-left corner. You'll draw like you were connecting the dots—click, click, click, double-click.

5   Following the illustration at the right, **click** at number 1 to begin drawing. When you release your mouse, you will notice a blue line connected to your cursor. This indicates you are in "drawing mode." Move your cursor to number 2 and **click**, then move to number 3 and **click**, move to number 4 and **double-click** to close the patch.

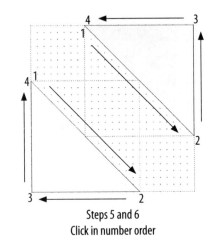
Steps 5 and 6
Click in number order

6   *Repeat step 5* to draw the half-square triangle in the other corner of the block.

> **Note**
> Patches should fill with cream when you double-click to close a shape. If the "Auto fill patch" option is not turned on, click BLOCK > Drawing Board Setup > Options > under Join and fill options, click Auto fill when patch is closed > OK.

7   Next, we'll follow the graph paper lines to draw a square in the center of the block. **Click** at any corner of the square, work clockwise or counter-clockwise, **clicking on each corner** as you go around and **end with a double-click** at the same point you began to close the patch.

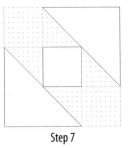
Step 7

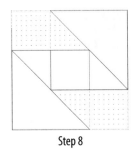
Step 8

8   Draw two triangle patches—one on the left and one on the right side of the square.

9   Draw two shapes in the remaining blank areas to complete the block.

10   Click **Add to Sketchbook** to save the block.

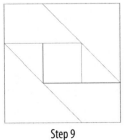
Step 9

Step 10
Add to Sketchbook

That was easy! See how fast you can build a block just by connecting the dots, so to speak? The graph paper is very helpful when you build a rectangular block because you know the grid points are at the intersections of the graph paper divisions.

20   EQ6 Pieced Drawing

Chapter 1: Click and Draw Blocks with Pieced PatchDraw

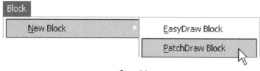

Step 11

Step 12

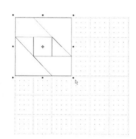

Step 13

Step 14
Pick

Now, let's try a variation of *Garret Windows*, but this time let's make it into a four patch block.

11 Click **BLOCK > New Block > PatchDraw Block** on the top menu bar to place a new PatchDraw block on the worktable.

12 We'll use the same settings on the Precision Bar as in step 3, except make this change:

- Cells Horizontal = **6**
- Cells Vertical = **6**

13 In the upper-left quadrant of the block, draw the *Garret Windows* block just as we did in the first part of this exercise.

14 Click the **Pick** tool.

> **Note**
> You can quickly switch back and forth between the Polydraw tools and the Pick tool by pressing the SPACEBAR on your keyboard.

15 **Point the cursor** at an area *just above the left corner of the block*. **Click and drag** diagonally to form a selection box (marquee) around the *Garret Windows* patches you just drew. All patches should be selected.

16 While the patches are still selected, click the **Clone** button on the Precision Bar. This makes a clone (copy) of the patch.

Step 16
Clone

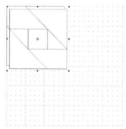

Step 15
Drag diagonally to form selection box

Step 16
Clone of selection

Companion Book Three

17 While the clone is still selected, click the **Rotate** button *twice*. The clone rotates 45 degrees with each click and is now rotated 90 degrees. Click and hold the center four-headed arrows and **drag** these patches to the top-right quadrant and keep them selected.

Step 17
Rotate

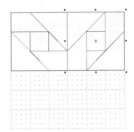
Step 17
Drag to top-right quadrant

18 *Repeat* the clone and double-rotate action two more times, moving one clone to the lower-right quadrant and the other clone to the lower-left quadrant.

Notice how easily the patches snap into place in Pieced PatchDraw—almost like you were placing them on a magnetic board!

19 Click **Add to Sketchbook**. This is your *Garrett Windows Variation* block.

Note
When you name your block on the Sketchbook Notecard, include *PatchDraw* in its name. Later, when you want to search for your Pieced PatchDraw blocks, you can do a search for "PatchDraw" and easily find them as a group.

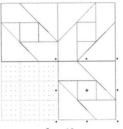
Step 18
Drag to lower-right quadrant

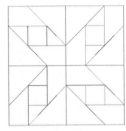
Step 18
Drag to lower-left quadrant

Step 19
Add to Sketchbook

Chapter 1: Click and Draw Blocks with Pieced PatchDraw

Show & Draw Rectangle Grid

Now that you've gone over the basics of the special Rectangle grid, exercise your mouse some more and try one of these blocks. Almost any traditional pieced blocks with straight line patches can be drawn on the Pieced PatchDraw Rectangle grid. This is just a sampling of some of the blocks I created on the Rectangle grid. Try one or try them all!

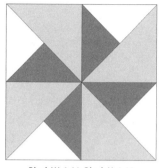

Block W: 8.00, Block H: 8.00
Snap H: 8, Snap V: 8
Graph Paper H: 8, Graph Paper V: 8

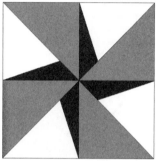

Block W: 8.00, Block H: 8.00
Snap H: 8, Snap V: 8
Graph Paper H: 8, Graph Paper V: 8

Block W: 4.00, Block H: 4.00
Snap H: 4, Snap V: 4
Graph Paper H: 4, Graph Paper V: 4
Tip: Use flip buttons for asymmetrical blocks

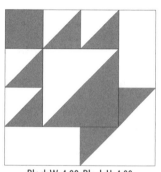

Block W: 4.00, Block H: 4.00
Snap H: 4, Snap V: 4
Graph Paper H: 4, Graph Paper V: 4
Tip: Use flip buttons for asymmetrical blocks

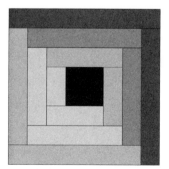

Block W: 8.00, Block H: 8.00
Snap H: 8, Snap V: 8
Graph Paper H: 8, Graph Paper V: 8
Tip: Logs are 1"

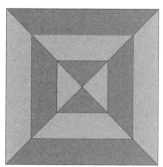

Block W: 6.00, Block H: 6.00
Snap H: 6, Snap V: 6
Graph Paper H: 6, Graph Paper V: 6

Block W: 16.00, Block H: 20.00
Snap H: 16, Snap V: 20
Graph Paper H: 16, Graph Paper V: 20
Tip: 1" logs frame an 8 x 10 center – great picture frame!

Companion Book Three

Chapter 1: Click and Draw Blocks with Pieced PatchDraw

Pieced PatchDraw Rectangle

Block W: 8.00, Block H: 8.00
Snap H: 24, Snap V: 24
Graph Paper H: 4, Graph Paper V: 4
Tip: Repeater block

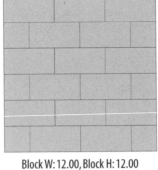

Block W: 12.00, Block H: 12.00
Snap H: 24, Snap V: 24
Graph Paper H: 12, Graph Paper V: 12
Tip: Repeater block

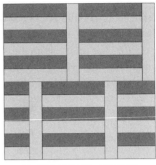

Block W: 12.00, Block H: 12.00
Snap H: 24, Snap V: 24
Graph Paper H: 12, Graph Paper V: 12
Tip: Repeater block

Block W: 12.00, Block H: 12.00
Snap H: 24, Snap V: 24
Graph Paper H: 12, Graph Paper V: 12
Tip: Draw triangles first

Block W: 8.00, Block H: 8.00
Snap H: 24, Snap V: 24
Graph Paper H: 8, Graph Paper V: 8
Tip: Repeater block

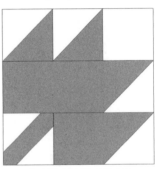

Block W: 6.00, Block H: 6.00
Snap H: 12, Snap V: 12
Graph Paper H: 6, Graph Paper V: 6
Tip: Easy foundation pattern

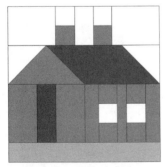

Block W: 8.00, Block H: 8.00
Snap H: 32, Snap V: 32
Graph Paper H: 8, Graph Paper V: 8
Tip: Change graph paper to 32 x 32 for small patches

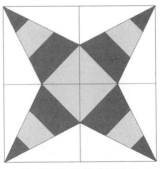

Block W: 12.00, Block H: 12.00
Snap H: 24, Snap V: 24
Graph Paper H: 12, Graph Paper V: 12
Tip: Stripes must fall on grid points

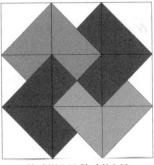

Block W: 9.00, Block H: 9.00
Snap H: 18, Snap V: 18
Graph Paper H: 9, Graph Paper V: 9

Chapter 1: Click and Draw Blocks with Pieced PatchDraw

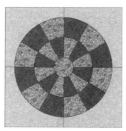

Example of *Pieced PatchDraw Circle* Block

Step 3

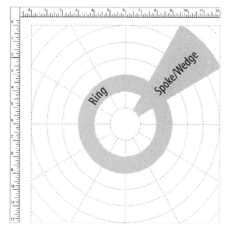

Circle Drawing Board

Step 4

Polydraw Tools

Step 5
PolyArc

Pieced PatchDraw Circle

Welcome to the world of drawing on a circular grid! In EQ6 the Pieced PatchDraw Circle grid opens a whole new way of drawing circle-based quilt blocks. No partitioning of arcs is needed and no math is required! Decide on the number of spokes and rings you want and you are ready to draw. Let's try a fancy wheel block to practice drawing on the circular grid.

Wheel-type blocks

1. Click **WORKTABLE > Work on Block**.

2. Click **BLOCK > New Block > PatchDraw Block**.

3. On the Precision Bar, enter these values pressing your keyboard TAB key after each:

    - Block Width = **12.00**
    - Block Height = **12.00**
    - Grid: **Circle**
    - Rings* = **6**
    - Spokes* = **12**
    - Graph Paper visibility is toggled **OFF**

    *see illustration
    Notice we have turned the graph paper visibility off. We don't need these square divisions when we draw circular blocks.

4. Make sure you are working on the **Pieced** tab of the PatchDraw block and not the Appliqué.

5. **Click and hold** on the **Polydraw** tool to make the PolyLine and PolyArc tools appear on the flyout. Click the **PolyArc** tool.

Companion Book Three **25**

Chapter 1: Click and Draw Blocks with Pieced PatchDraw

Pieced PatchDraw Circle

The PolyArc tool is used for drawing on the Circle and the Arc special grids. You can draw straight lines as well as circular ones using this tool.

6   Begin by drawing a 2" circle in the center of the block. Start at any spoke around the center grid circle, click on each intersection going in a clockwise direction. **Double-click** when you reach the same point where you began to close the shape.

Notice how the lines automatically bend to the curve after you make the next click! This special bending will be even more apparent as you draw patches further away from the center of the circular grid.

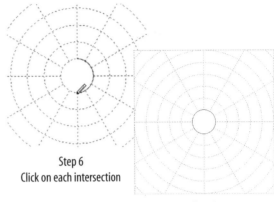

Step 6
Click on each intersection

Step 6
Double-click to close shape

> **Note**
> When using the PolyArc tool around curves, the more clicks or nodes you add the better. This is necessary to make a smoother, more accurate curve. If you skip intersections when tracing around a curve it may leave gaps in your drawing. For example if you have the circular grid set up with twelve spokes, click at all twelve spoke intersections when you draw a circle.

7   Working in the wedge area to the right of the spoke at 12:00 (12 o'clock), draw a blade shape two rings high from the center circle.

8   Draw another two-ring high blade shape on top of this.

9   Press the **SPACEBAR** to switch to the **Pick** tool.

10 Click and drag diagonally to make a selection marquee around the two blades to select them both.

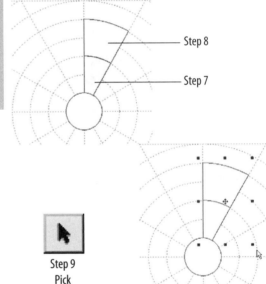

Step 9
Pick

Step 10
Drag diagonally to form selection box

26   EQ6 Pieced Drawing

Chapter 1: Click and Draw Blocks with Pieced PatchDraw

Step 11
Clone

Step 11
Rotate

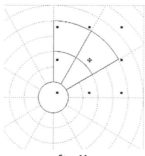

Step 11
Drag to the right of first set of blades

11   On the Precision Bar, click the **Clone** button > **Rotate** button > **drag** the patch to the right of the first patch of blades.

12   With the cloned patches still selected, click the **Clone** button > **Rotate** button. *Repeat* this process (Clone > Rotate) *10 more times* to create a wheel of 12 double blades.

Notice how EQ6 knows just how much to rotate the patches! This particular Circle grid has twelve 30 degree wedges. But guess what? You don't need to know any math to create this block!

13   Press the **SPACEBAR** to switch back to the **PolyArc** tool.

Now let's draw the background around the wheel. For this block we'll create the background in four separate sections.

14   Beginning at the top-center of the block at 12:00, draw around the background area in the upper-right quadrant. Basically you will be tracing around the area not yet covered with patches. When you click around the side next to the wheel, click at points where the spokes meet the wheel. It takes only eight quick clicks to get back to the starting point. When you get back to the point where you began the patch, **double-click** to close the patch.

Note how patches are automatically selected after you double-click to close them. If you just need to rotate or clone one patch you can do this without switching to the Pick tool. But also note that the PolyArc tool is still active.

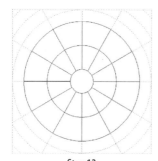

Step 12
Wheel of 12 double blades

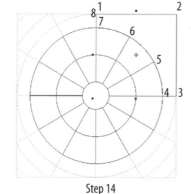

Step 13
PolyArc

Step 14

Companion Book Three   **27**

Chapter 1: Click and Draw Blocks with Pieced PatchDraw

15. So with the patch still selected, click the **Clone** button > **Rotate** button *three* times to rotate it 90 degrees. Move this clone to the bottom right-quadrant.

16. While each successive cloned patch is still selected, *repeat* **Clone** > *triple* **Rotate** *two more times*, moving each clone into its corresponding quadrant to complete the block.

17. Click **Add to Sketchbook**.

Step 15
Clone

Step 15
Rotate

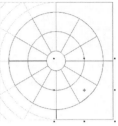
Step 15
Drag to bottom-right quadrant

> **Note**
> The Symmetry box is available if you want to use it to clone, rotate or flip patches. It is only available if patches are selected with the Pick tool. With a patch or patches selected, on the BLOCK menu, click on Symmetry. Most of the time you will not need to use the Symmetry box as it is usually quicker to use the buttons on the Precision bar.

Step 16

Step 17
Add to Sketchbook

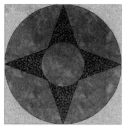

Example of *Compass* Block

Compass-type blocks

Now that you have learned how to draw a wheel on the Circle grid, let's put together a simple compass block so that you can practice drawing star points. You're going to love how easy this is!

1   Click **WORKTABLE > Work on Block**.

2   Click **BLOCK > New Block > PatchDraw Block.**

3   On the Precision Bar, enter these values pressing your keyboard TAB key after each:

   - Block Width = **8.00**
   - Block Height = **8.00**
   - Grid: **Circle**
   - Rings = **8**
   - Spokes = **16**
   - Graph Paper visibility is toggled **OFF**

4   **Click and hold** on the **Polydraw** tool to make the PolyLine and PolyArc tools appear on the flyout. Click the **PolyArc** tool.

5   First draw the circle patch in the center of the compass. Count two rings out from the center and begin drawing the circle at 12:00. Work clockwise by clicking around the circle on each grid intersection. **Double-click** when you get back to the starting point to close the patch (17 clicks).

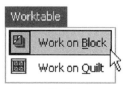

Step 1

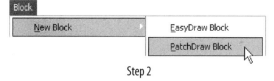

Step 2

Step 3

Polydraw Tools   Step 4
                    PolyArc

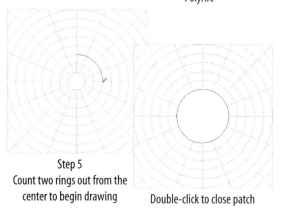

Step 5
Count two rings out from the center to begin drawing

Double-click to close patch

Chapter 1: Click and Draw Blocks with Pieced PatchDraw

6. Draw the first star point from the top-center of the block to the second spoke intersection to the left of 12:00 on the center circle patch. Click around the top of the circle at each intersection and when you get to the second spoke to the right of 12:00 go back up to the top-center of the block where you began. **Double-click** to close the patch.

7. With the patch still selected, click **Clone > Rotate** *four times* and place the clone on the East side of the center. *Repeat* two more times until you have four compass points around the center (North, South, East and West).

> **Note**
> **If your patch takes up more than one wedge between spokes, click the Rotate button that many times to rotate a clone to the next matching area on the Circle grid. For example, if I draw a star point patch that crosses over two wedges, I click the Rotate button twice, or if I cross over four wedges, I click Rotate four times.**

8. Draw the curved background patch between the star points in the upper-right quarter of the block, clicking around the area between the two star points. Remember to click at spoke intersections around the outer curve to keep the curve smooth.

9. Draw the remaining part of the background in this quarter, clicking around the curve of the previous patch and around the corner of the block. You might find it easier to begin at the upper-right corner of the block and work your way around the patch. Be sure to click at the narrow area at the top- and right-center of the block (at the tip of the star point) to make the complete patch.

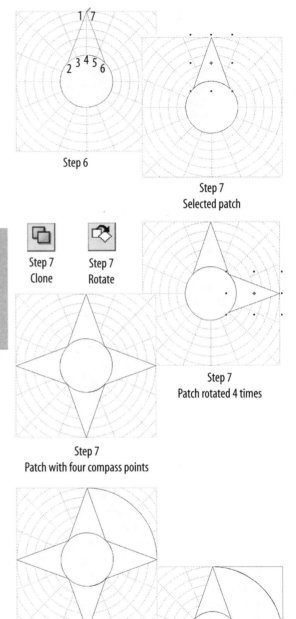

Step 6

Step 7
Selected patch

Step 7
Clone

Step 7
Rotate

Step 7
Patch rotated 4 times

Step 7
Patch with four compass points

Step 8

Step 9

Chapter 1: Click and Draw Blocks with Pieced PatchDraw

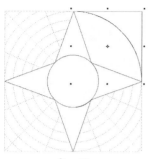

Step 10
Select both background patches

Step 10
Clone

Step 10
Rotate

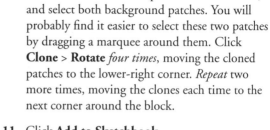

10. Switch to the **Pick** tool (press the **SPACEBAR**) and select both background patches. You will probably find it easier to select these two patches by dragging a marquee around them. Click **Clone** > **Rotate** *four times*, moving the cloned patches to the lower-right corner. *Repeat* two more times, moving the clones each time to the next corner around the block.

11. Click **Add to Sketchbook.**

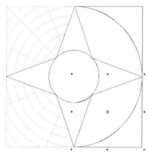

Step 10
Move cloned patches to lower-right corner

> **Notes**
> - There is no set order when you draw the patches, so don't feel you must draw them in the same order as I do! Sometimes I do not know where I am headed when I am drawing a compass design, so I may draw and rotate the longest points first and then go back and fill in the shapes between these, rotating as I go. Other times I may draw the center first and work my way around the block. Do whatever works easiest for you and your block.
>
> - To make a more foundation-friendly pattern, try using the PolyLine tool on the Circle and Arc grids. Keep in mind that you are still limited to snap points on ring/spoke intersections, so usually you must draw the background patches in sections to match the wedges in the main design.

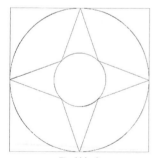

Final block

Step 11
Add to Sketchbook

Chapter 1: Click and Draw Blocks with Pieced PatchDraw

Show & Draw Circle Grid

Click your way to a Sketchbook full of circular blocks! All you need to get started on these is the size, rings and spokes. Some of the circles fill the block and some have more background—feel free to vary the designs as you like. Two of the stars I drew with just the PolyLine tool, creating a block that can easily be foundation pieced. Note that when you draw a circular block with all straight lines you will need to section the background.

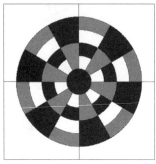

Block W: 12.00, Block H: 12.00
Rings: 6
Spokes: 12

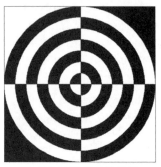

Block W: 14.00, Block H: 14.00
Rings: 7
Spokes: 4

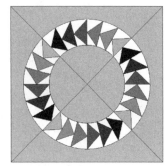

Block W: 12.00, Block H: 12.00
Rings: 12
Spokes: 24
Tip: Draw one quarter block first

Block W: 8.00, Block H: 8.00
Rings: 8
Spokes: 20
Tip: Background patches follow the star wedge lines

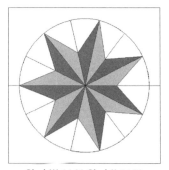

Block W: 14.00, Block H: 14.00
Rings: 7
Spokes: 14
Tip: It's easier to make the background in two pieces for 7-point stars

Block W: 16.00, Block H: 16.00
Rings: 8
Spokes: 48
Tip: Bottom corners of secondary points must be on spoke/ring intersection

Block W: 16.00, Block H: 16.00
Rings: 8
Spokes: 16
Tip: Bottom corners of secondary points must be on spoke/ring intersection

Chapter 1: Click and Draw Blocks with Pieced PatchDraw

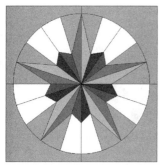

Block W: 10.00, Block H: 10.00
Rings: 10
Spokes: 20

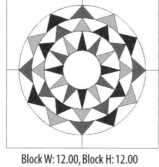

Block W: 12.00, Block H: 12.00
Rings: 12
Spokes: 24
Tip: 3" center circle

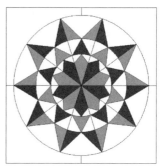

Block W: 10.00, Block H: 10.00
Rings: 10
Spokes: 20

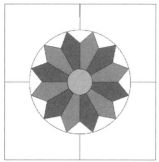

Block W: 12.00, Block H: 12.00
Rings: 12
Spokes: 24

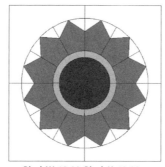

Block W: 12.00, Block H: 12.00
Rings: 12
Spokes: 24
Tip: 4" center circle

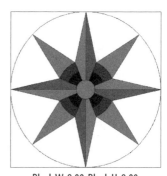

Block W: 8.00, Block H: 8.00
Rings: 8
Spokes: 16
Tip: Draw half top star point, clone & flip. 1" center circle

Block W: 8.00, Block H: 8.00
Rings: 8
Spokes: 16
Tip: Use PolyLine tool only
(all lines are straight)

Block W: 16.00, Block H: 16.00
Rings: 16
Spokes: 32
Tip: 3" center circle

Block W: 10.00, Block H: 10.00
Rings: 10
Spokes: 20
Tip: Use PolyLine tool only
(all lines are straight)

Pieced PatchDraw Circle

Companion Book Three

Pieced PatchDraw Arc

The Pieced PatchDraw Arc grid is another circular grid—but only one quarter of a circle. It's great for fans and sun compass-type blocks. In this exercise, we'll draw a variation of the *New York Beauty* block. This block is a little more adventurous, but I know you will love it!

1   Click **WORKTABLE > Work on Block**.

2   Click **BLOCK > New Block > PatchDraw Block**.

Example of *New York Beauty* Block

Step 3

3   On the Precision Bar, enter these values pressing your keyboard TAB key after each:

- Block Width = **9.00**
- Block Height = **9.00**
- Grid: **Arc**
- Rings* = **9**
- Spokes* = **10**
- Graph Paper visibility is toggled **OFF**

*see illustration

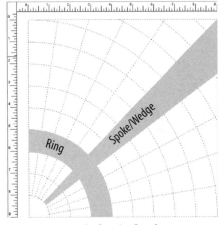

Arc Drawing Board

> **Note**
> Usually I like to make the number of rings the same as the block size. That way my rings are 1" apart. It does not mean you have to print the block that size, but just like the graph paper divisions on a rectangular block, knowing ring size can be very helpful when drawing the block.

4   **Click and hold** on the **Polydraw** tool to make the PolyLine and PolyArc tools appear on the flyout. Click the **PolyArc** tool.

Polydraw Tools   Step 4
                        PolyArc

We'll begin by drawing a quarter circle in the block's lower-left corner.

5   **Click 6" down on the left side** of the block (so you will end up with a 3" quarter circle). Remember to **click at each spoke intersection** when you draw around the curve, for a nice smooth curve. **Double-click** to close the patch.

Step 5   Step 5
Click on each   Double-click to close shape
intersection

Chapter 1: Click and Draw Blocks with Pieced PatchDraw

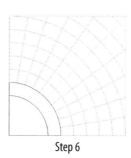

Step 6

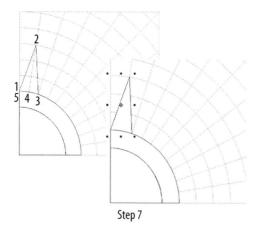

Step 7

Step 8 Clone   Step 8 Rotate

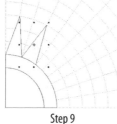

Step 9

Step 10 Clone   Step 10 Rotate

Step 10

6. Draw a rainbow-shaped patch in the next ring out from the quarter circle. This one will take quite a few more clicks, but it goes really fast since the special snap to grid is at work!

   Our *New York Beauty* block is going to have five star points. Each star point will be two wedges wide at its base and three rings tall. Sound difficult? It's not! We only have to draw one star point and then clone and rotate will do the rest.

7. Working in the first two wedges on the left, draw the first star point. **Click at the left-top point** of the previous rainbow patch, go up three rings and over to the first spoke, **click**. Continue clicking to draw the other half of the star point and then go back around the curve, clicking on the spoke intersection and then back to where you began. **Double-click** to close the patch.

8. While the star point patch is still selected, click **Clone** > click **Rotate** *twice* (two wedges = two rotations).

9. Drag this cloned patch to the right of the original star point patch.

10. *Repeat* this process three more times (**Clone > double-Rotate > drag the patch**) moving each clone to the next wedge section.

Companion Book Three **35**

11 To the right of the first star point, draw the triangular background patch.

12 Click **Clone > double-Rotate**. Move the patch to the next space between star points. *Repeat this process two more times* (**Clone > double-Rotate > drag the patch**).

13 Draw patches in the two remaining end areas for this ring of patches.

14 Draw another rainbow-shaped patch. Remember to click on all the spoke intersections as you go around the curve.

15 To complete the block, draw a patch in the remaining background area.

16 Click **Add to Sketchbook** to save your *New York Beauty* block.

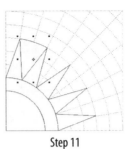

Step 12 Clone

Step 12 Rotate

Step 11

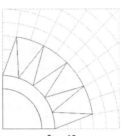
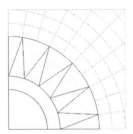

Step 12

Step 13

Step 14

Step 15

Step 16
Add to Sketchbook

Show & Draw Arc Grid

Although you may want use your fan block by itself, try setting it in a 2 x 2 horizontal quilt layout, rotating the blocks so that they make a full circle. You might also want to try the Symmetry tool on the quilt worktable—play with it and see what happens!

Block W: 9.00, Block H: 9.00
Rings: 9
Spokes: 10

Block W: 12.00, Block H: 12.00
Rings: 10
Spokes: 10

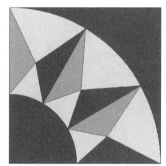

Block W: 9.00, Block H: 9.00
Rings: 9
Spokes: 12

Block W: 9.00, Block H: 9.00
Rings: 9
Spokes: 12

Block W: 9.00, Block H: 9.00
Rings: 9
Spokes: 8
Tip: Color the "spirals" for a Giant Dahlia look!

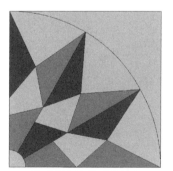

Block W: 9.00, Block H: 9.00
Rings: 9
Spokes: 12
Tip: Odd angles still need to snap to intersections

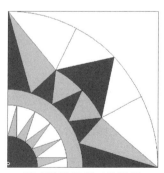

Block W: 10.00, Block H: 10.00
Rings: 10
Spokes: 10
Tip: Set four of these together for full effect

Pieced PatchDraw Arc

Companion Book Three **37**

Chapter 1: Click and Draw Blocks with Pieced PatchDraw

Pieced PatchDraw Arc

Block W: 12.00, Block H: 12.00
Rings: 10
Spokes: 10
Tip: Careful coloring makes the fan folds

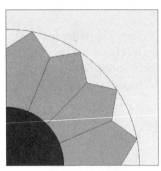

Block Width: 8.00
Block Height: 8.00
Rings: 8
Spokes: 16

Block W: 8.00, Block H: 8.00
Rings: 8
Spokes: 16
Tip: Draw one pair and rotate together

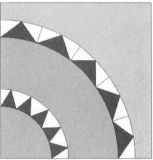

Block W: 9.00, Block H: 9.00
Rings: 9
Spokes: 10

Block W: 12.00, Block H: 12.00
Rings: 8
Spokes: 8
Tip: Work on one ring at a time

Block W: 8.00, Block H: 8.00
Rings: 8
Spokes: 16

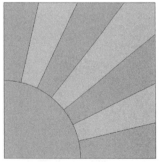

Block W: 12.00, Block H: 12.00
Rings: 4
Spokes: 14
Tip: Draw each wedge separately

Block W: 12.00, Block H: 12.00
Rings: 10
Spokes: 12
Tip: Create two wedges and rotate together

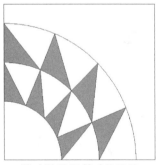

Block W: 12.00, Block H: 12.00
Rings: 8
Spokes: 8
Tip: Set four of these together for full effect

Chapter 1: Click and Draw Blocks with Pieced PatchDraw

Example of *LeMoyne Star* Block

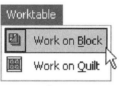

Step 1

Step 2

Step 3

Pieced PatchDraw Eight-Point Star

The *Eight-Point Star* block (also known as *LeMoyne Star*) is one of the most popular blocks in quilting. Perhaps that's because it's a perfect candidate for creating variations. Popular block or not, it is not an easy block to draw on a square grid. However, Pieced PatchDraw provides a special grid just for this star—perfect 45 degree angles are already built into the grid!

In this exercise let's draw a three-dimensional *LeMoyne Star* block. The beauty of doing it in Pieced PatchDraw is that we only need to draw one portion, since Clone and Rotate can do the rest.

1 Click **WORKTABLE > Work on Block.**

2 Click **BLOCK > New Block > PatchDraw Block**.

3 On the Precision Bar, enter these values pressing your keyboard TAB key after each:

- Block Width = **12.00**
- Block Height = **12.00**
- Grid: **Eight Point Star**
- Dimension 1 = **5**
- Dimension 2 = **5**
- Graph Paper visibility is toggled **OFF**

The dimensions of the Eight Point Star grid refer to the divisions of the diamonds and the background areas. The divisions in the corner squares are horizontal and vertical. Inside the diamonds and the triangles the divisions are at 45 degree angles.

Notice also that the grid inside the background squares and triangles is made up of squares. The grid inside the diamonds is made up of diamonds. However, these grids line up perfectly wherever the diamonds meet the background.

4 **Click and hold** on the **Polydraw** tool to make the PolyLine and PolyArc tools appear on the flyout. Click the **PolyLine** tool.

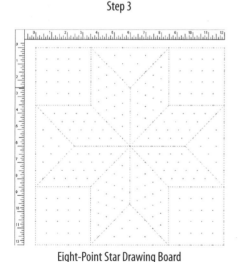

Eight-Point Star Drawing Board

Polydraw Tools

Step 4
PolyLine

Companion Book Three **39**

Chapter 1: Click and Draw Blocks with Pieced PatchDraw

5   In the top-left diamond, draw a patch that divides the diamond in half.

6   Draw another mirror image half-diamond next to it.

7   Press your keyboard **SPACEBAR** to switch to the **Pick** tool.

8   Click **EDIT > Select all** on the top menu bar to select both halves of the diamond.

9   Click the **Clone** button > click the **Rotate** button > **drag** the clone to the next diamond space to the right.

10 Press your keyboard **SPACEBAR** to switch back to the **PolyLine** tool.

11 Draw the top-center triangle.

12 While this triangle patch is still selected, click the **Clone** button > click the **Rotate** button > **drag** the clone to the lower-left corner of the upper-right background square.

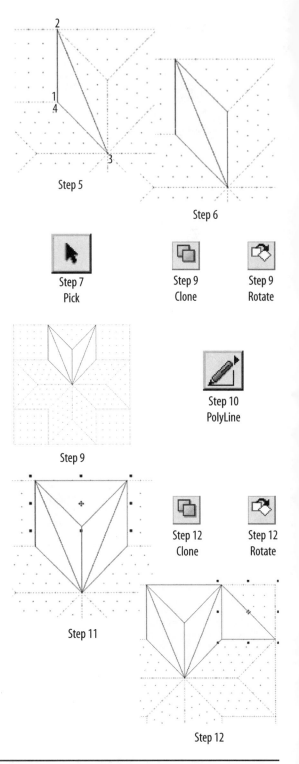

40   EQ6 Pieced Drawing

Chapter 1: Click and Draw Blocks with Pieced PatchDraw

Step 13
Flip left and right

Step 13
Flip top and bottom

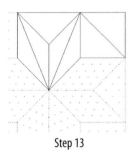

Step 13

13. Click **Clone** > click the **Flip left and right** button > click the **Flip top and bottom** button > **drag** the triangle to the upper-right corner.

14. Click the **Pick** tool.

15. Hold down your keyboard **CTRL** key as you press the **A** key (**CTRL+A** = Select all) to select all the patches.

16. Click **Clone** > click **Rotate** *twice* to rotate the patches 90 degrees > **drag** them to the bottom-right side of the block.

17. **Clone** and **double-rotate** each successive group of patches *two more times* moving each clone to the adjacent section (going clockwise).

Done! Isn't that amazing how fast you can draw this block?

18. Click **Add to Sketchbook** to save your block.

Step 14
Pick

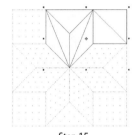

Step 15

Step 16
Clone

Step 16
Rotate

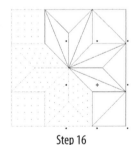

Step 16

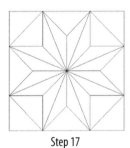

Step 17

Step 18
Add to Sketchbook

Companion Book Three **41**

Chapter 1: Click and Draw Blocks with Pieced PatchDraw

Make it Foundation-Friendly!

Eight-point stars can sometimes be a challenge to stitch together. Let me show you how easy it is to take this Pieced PatchDraw eight-point star block we created and make it so that it's "foundation-friendly." In other words, we'll edit the existing block so that we can print an easy-to-stitch foundation pattern.

Step 19
View Sketchbook

19   Click on the **View Sketchbook** button.

20   In the Sketchbook, select the star block saved in step 18. Click on **Edit** to place the block on the worktable. You should be on the **Pieced** layer of PatchDraw when you do this.

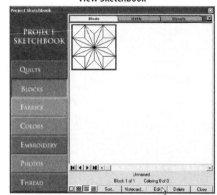

Step 20

To make the eight-point star easier to foundation piece we need to change the seam lines in the background patches so that they make a continuous seam with the star patches in the center of the block. We can do that by rotating some of the background patches, and for the rest we can redraw them to create new seam lines.

21   Click on the **Pick** tool. Drag a marquee around the corner half-square triangles in the upper-left of the block.

22   While the triangles are selected, click on the **Rotate** button *twice* to rotate them 90 degrees. Rotating them may move the patches slightly off the grid, so while they are still selected move them so that they snap back into place. *Repeat* this process (select and rotate) in the remaining three corners. Now the diagonal of the rotated triangles makes a continuous line with diagonal of the star.

We also need to change the background triangles between the star points.

23   With the **Pick** tool, select and then press your keyboard **DELETE** key for each of the four triangles between the star points.

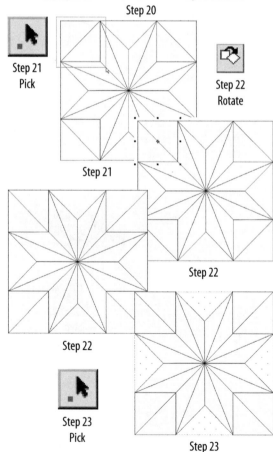

42   EQ6 Pieced Drawing

Chapter 1: Click and Draw Blocks with Pieced PatchDraw

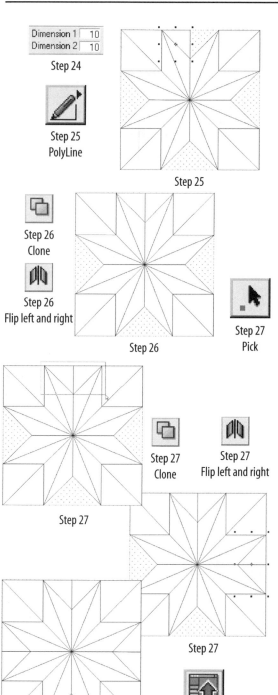

24 On the Precision Bar, change both the Dimension 1 and Dimension 2 to **10**. Press **ENTER** on your keyboard to see the change. We need to change these dimensions so that there is a snap point in the center.

25 Click on the **PolyLine** tool. Starting at the top-center of the block in the blank space between the star points, draw a half-triangle on the left.

26 While the new triangle is still selected, click on **Clone** and then **Flip left and right** button. Move the flipped clone to fill the other half of the space.

27 Click the **Pick** tool. Drag a marquee around both half-triangles to select them. Click on **Clone** and then click on the **Rotate** button *twice* to rotate them 90 degrees. Move these to the corresponding space on the right side of the block. *Repeat* this process (**Clone > double-rotate**) *twice* to fill the remaining two spaces on the block.

28 **Add the block to the Sketchbook** when you're done.

That's all there is to it! To see the difference these changes made, compare the foundation pattern with that of the original block. **Click FILE > Print > Foundation Pattern** and then compare the units indicated by the blue lines on the Sections tab. For the original block EQ sees each star point and background section as a separate unit! That might be okay for hand-piecing, but we know it's not easy to foundation piece. For our edited foundation-friendly block there are eight equally divided units. Each unit can be foundation pieced and then the units can easily be stitched together to make the block.

You can apply this same idea to make other Pieced PatchDraw blocks foundation-friendly. The most important thing to remember is that when you edit the block, change the patches in a way so that they create a continuous seam line to the block outline.

Companion Book Three

Chapter 1: Click and Draw Blocks with Pieced PatchDraw

Show & Draw Eight Point Star Grid

When you're trying all the fancy eight-point stars don't forget to try the traditional *LeMoyne Star* block! I concentrated on the star itself in this sampling of blocks for you to try, but feel free to vary the background to suit yourself. By the way, if you love LeMoyne-type star blocks you may also want to see the last chapter of this book and learn how to draw it in EasyDraw™ as well.

Block W: 6.00, Block H: 6.00
Dimension 1: 4, Dimension 2: 4

Block W: 12.00, Block H: 12.00
Dimension 1: 4, Dimension 2: 4

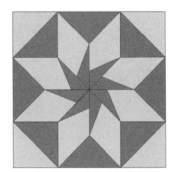

Block W: 12.00, Block H: 12.00
Dimension 1: 8, Dimension 2: 8

Block W: 12.00, Block H: 12.00
Dimension 1: 12, Dimension 2: 12

Block W: 12.00, Block H: 12.00
Dimension 1: 6, Dimension 2: 6
Tip: Foundation-friendly

Block W: 12.00, Block H: 12.00
Dimension 1: 2, Dimension 2: 2

Block W: 12.00, Block H: 12.00
Dimension 1: 3, Dimension 2: 3

Chapter 1: Click and Draw Blocks with Pieced PatchDraw

Block W: 12.00, Block H: 12.00
Dimension 1: 5, Dimension 2: 5

Block W: 12.00, Block H: 12.00
Dimension 1: 2, Dimension 2: 2

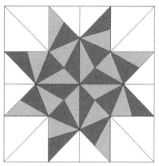

Block W: 6.00, Block H: 6.00
Dimension 1: 4, Dimension 2: 4
Tip: Foundation-friendly

Block W: 6.00, Block H: 6.00
Dimension 1: 4, Dimension 2: 4
Tip: Center is an octagon

Block W: 12.00, Block H: 12.00
Dimension 1: 8, Dimension 2: 8
Tip: Set in quilt layout for full effect

Block W: 12.00, Block H: 12.00
Dimension 1: 4, Dimension 2: 4
Tip: Foundation-friendly

Block W: 12.00, Block H: 12.00
Dimension 1: 4, Dimension 2: 4
Tip: Half-diamonds make feathers!

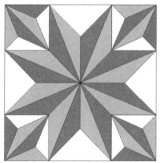

Block W: 12.00, Block H: 12.00
Dimension 1: 10, Dimension 2: 10
Tip: Set in quilt layout for full effect

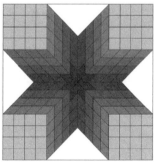

Block W: 12.00, Block H: 12.00
Dimension 1: 8, Dimension 2: 8
Tip: Color with shades of four different hues

Pieced PatchDraw Eight-Point Star

Companion Book Three

Chapter 1: Click and Draw Blocks with Pieced PatchDraw

Pieced PatchDraw Kaleidoscope

The Pieced PatchDraw Kaleidoscope grid gives us with another grid based on 45 degree shapes. Let's draw a traditional *Kaleidoscope* block called *Concord*.

1. Click **WORKTABLE > Work on Block**.

2. Click **BLOCK > New Block > PatchDraw Block**.

Example of *Concord* Block

3. On the Precision Bar, enter these values pressing your keyboard TAB key after each:

   - Block Width = **12.00**
   - Block Height = **12.00**
   - Grid: **Kaleidoscope**
   - Dimension 1 = **6**
   - Dimension 2 = **6**
   - Graph Paper visibility is toggled **ON**
   - Cells Horizontal = **2**
   - Cells Vertical = **2**

Step 3

We're turning on the graph paper for this block so we can have a visible center line.

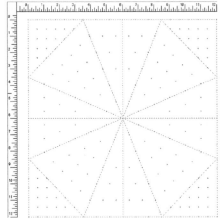

Kaleidoscope Drawing Board

4. **Click and hold** on the **Polydraw** tool to make the PolyLine and PolyArc tools appear on the flyout. Click the **PolyLine** tool.

We'll draw an upright diamond in the top-center wedge.

Polydraw Tools

Step 4
PolyLine

5. **Click** first at the top-center of the block > count down three grid points diagonally and make the second **click** > **click** at the center of the block > count up three, **click** and then **click** at the point where you began > **double-click** to close the patch.

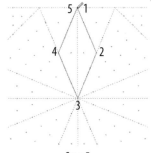

Step 5

46 EQ6 Pieced Drawing

Chapter 1: Click and Draw Blocks with Pieced PatchDraw

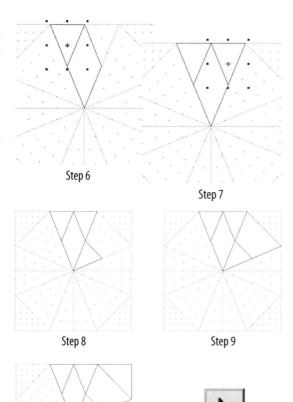

Step 6

Step 7

6. Draw the triangle patch to the left of the diamond. While the patch is still selected, do the next step.

7. Click **Clone** > **drag** the clone to the right of the diamond.

8. Click **Clone** again > click **Rotate** > **drag** this rotated triangle to place it in the adjacent wedge, with the bottom point at the center of the block.

9. Draw the pyramid shape above this triangle.

10. Draw the corner triangle patch.

11. Press your keyboard **SPACEBAR** to switch to the **Pick** tool.

12. Use **CTRL+A** to select all.

13. Click **Clone** > click **Rotate** *twice* to rotate the patches 90 degrees > **drag** them to the bottom-right side of the block.

Step 8

Step 9

Step 11
Pick

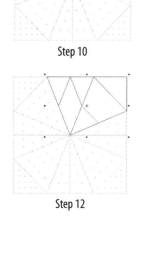

Step 10

Step 13
Clone

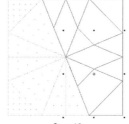

Step 13
Rotate

Step 12

Step 13

Companion Book Three **47**

Chapter 1: Click and Draw Blocks with Pieced PatchDraw

14. Click **Clone** > click **Rotate** *twice* > move the patches to the adjacent section.

15. Click **Clone** > click **Rotate** *twice* > move the patches to the final section to complete the block.

16. Click **Add to Sketchbook** to save your block.

> **Note**
> Here's a color tip—give your *Concord* block a transparent look by coloring the inner patches green and the other parts blue and yellow, for example.

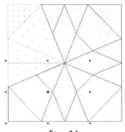

Step 14

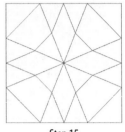

Step 15

Step 16
Add to Sketchbook

Show & Draw Kaleidoscope Grid

The Kaleidoscope grid has a lot of versatility. Fill the elongated triangle with diamonds to easily create eight-point stars or fill them with other shapes to create new designs. Since this grid also has 45 degree angles you can create alternating blocks to use in a quilt with eight-point star blocks. Here you'll find a little of both!

Block W: 12.00, Block H: 12.00
Dimension 1: 6, Dimension 2: 6

Block W: 12.00, Block H: 12.00
Dimension 1: 8, Dimension 2: 8

Block W: 12.00, Block H: 12.00
Dimension 1: 6, Dimension 2: 6

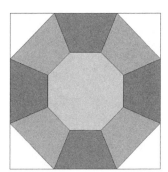

Block W: 12.00, Block H: 12.00
Dimension 1: 8, Dimension 2: 8

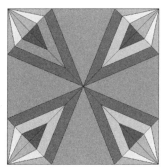

Block W: 12.00, Block H: 12.00
Dimension 1: 12, Dimension 2: 12

Block W: 12.00, Block H: 12.00
Dimension 1: 16, Dimension 2: 16
Tip: It only *looks* complex!

Block W: 12.00, Block H: 12.00
Dimension 1: 4, Dimension 2: 4

Companion Book Three 49

Chapter 1: Click and Draw Blocks with Pieced PatchDraw

Pieced PatchDraw Kaleidoscope

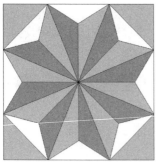

Block W: 12.00, Block H: 12.00
Dimension 1: 8, Dimension 2: 8

Block W: 12.00, Block H: 12.00
Dimension 1: 8, Dimension 2: 8

Block W: 12.00, Block H: 12.00
Dimension 1: 8, Dimension 2: 8

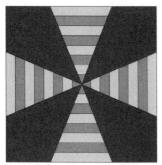

Block W: 12.00, Block H: 12.00
Dimension 1: 8, Dimension 2: 8

Block W: 12.00, Block H: 12.00
Dimension 1: 8, Dimension 2: 8
Tip: Good alternate block

Block W: 12.00, Block H: 12.00
Dimension 1: 8, Dimension 2: 8
Tip: Good alternate block

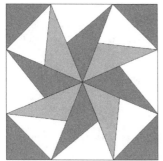

Block W: 12.00, Block H: 12.00
Dimension 1: 4, Dimension 2: 4
Tip: Foundation-friendly

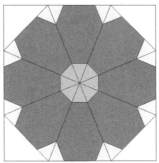

Block W: 12.00, Block H: 12.00
Dimension 1: 4, Dimension 2: 4
Tip: Foundation-friendly

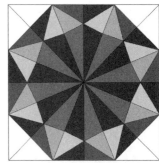

Block W: 12.00, Block H: 12.00
Dimension 1: 8, Dimension 2: 8
Tip: Foundation-friendly

Chapter 1: Click and Draw Blocks with Pieced PatchDraw

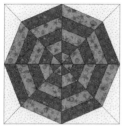

Example of *Pieced PatchDraw Octagon* Block

Step 3

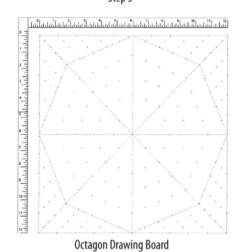

Octagon Drawing Board

Pieced PatchDraw Octagon

Another grid with 45 degree shapes! The octagon is set on-point creating a block that can be divided into four mirror-image quadrants. Let's use this grid to create a string-pieced block that looks like a spider web.

1 Click **WORKTABLE > Work on Block**.

2 Click **BLOCK > New Block > PatchDraw Block**.

3 On the Precision Bar, enter these values pressing your keyboard TAB key after each:

   - Block Width = **12.00**
   - Block Height = **12.00**
   - Grid: **Octagon**
   - Dimension 1 = **5**
   - Dimension 2 = **5**
   - Graph Paper visibility is toggled **OFF**

4 **Click and hold** on the **Polydraw** tool to make the PolyLine and PolyArc tools appear on the flyout. Click the **PolyLine** tool.

5 In the top-left wedge of the octagon, draw a small triangle in the bottom point.

6 In the same wedge, draw a strip patch in the next row of dots above the small triangle.

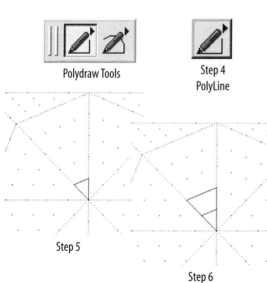

Polydraw Tools

Step 4 PolyLine

Step 5

Step 6

Companion Book Three

Chapter 1: Click and Draw Blocks with Pieced PatchDraw

Pieced PatchDraw Octagon

7   Draw three more strips in the same wedge out to the edge of the octagon.

8   Draw the patch for the skinny background triangle.

When you've finished this part, your patches fill a half-square triangle.

9   Press your keyboard **SPACEBAR** to switch to the **Pick** tool.

10 Use **CTRL+A** to select all.

11 Click **Clone** > click the **Flip left and right** button > **drag** these patches to the right of first ones, creating a mirror image pair. Click your mouse anywhere *off* the block to deselect the patches once they are in place.

12 Use **CTRL+A** > click **Clone** > click **Rotate** *twice* to rotate the patches 90 degrees > **drag** the cloned patches to the right side of the block. We'll repeat this twice in the next two steps. Your patches should still be selected.

13 Click **Clone** > click **Rotate** *twice* > **drag** the cloned patches to the adjacent part of the block.

14 Click **Clone** > click **Rotate** *twice* > **drag** the cloned patches to the adjacent part of the block.

15 Click **Add to Sketchbook** to save your block.

Challenge
With the skills you learned in the previous exercise with the Kaleidoscope grid, can you draw an *Octagon* block with an *Eight-Point Star* inside it? (Hint: Change the Dimension 1 and 2 to even numbers).

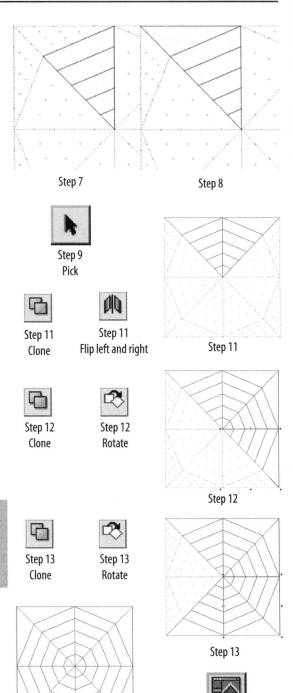

52   *EQ6 Pieced Drawing*

Chapter 1: Click and Draw Blocks with Pieced PatchDraw

Show & Draw Octagon Grid

Test your new Pieced PatchDraw skills on this batch of Octagons! The background of this octagon block when set side-by-side in a horizontal quilt layout creates a four-point star. You can change the background if you like as I did in a couple of these blocks. The secondary design you get when you set it in a quilt layout may surprise you!

Block W: 12.00, Block H: 12.00
Dimension 1: 6, Dimension 2: 6

Pieced PatchDraw Octagon

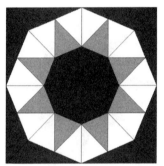

Block W: 12.00, Block H: 12.00
Dimension 1: 8, Dimension 2: 8

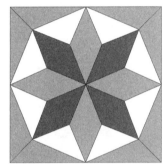

Block W: 12.00, Block H: 12.00
Dimension 1: 10, Dimension 2: 10

Block W: 12.00, Block H: 12.00
Dimension 1: 8, Dimension 2: 8

Block W: 12.00, Block H: 12.00
Dimension 1: 8, Dimension 2: 8

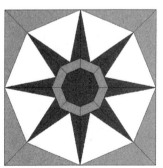

Block W: 12.00, Block H: 12.00
Dimension 1: 16, Dimension 2: 16

Block W: 12.00, Block H: 12.00
Dimension 1: 10, Dimension 2: 10
Tip: Foundation-friendly

Companion Book Three   53

Chapter 1: Click and Draw Blocks with Pieced PatchDraw

Pieced PatchDraw Octagon

Block W: 12.00, Block H: 12.00
Dimension 1: 8, Dimension 2: 8

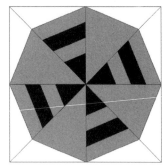

Block W: 12.00, Block H: 12.00
Dimension 1: 5, Dimension 2: 5

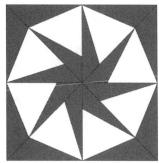

Block W: 12.00, Block H: 12.00
Dimension 1: 12, Dimension 2: 12

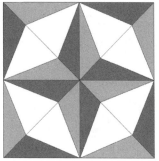

Block W: 12.00, Block H: 12.00
Dimension 1: 5, Dimension 2: 5

Block W: 12.00, Block H: 12.00
Dimension 1: 8, Dimension 2: 8

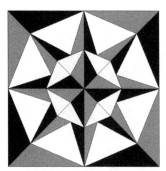

Block W: 12.00, Block H: 12.00
Dimension 1: 8, Dimension 2: 8

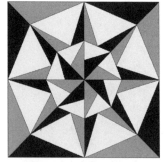

Block W: 12.00, Block H: 12.00
Dimension 1: 8, Dimension 2: 8
Tip: Flip dark side of inner star of previous block to make the pinwheel

Block W: 12.00, Block H: 12.00
Dimension 1: 8, Dimension 2: 8
Tip: Set in quilt layout for full effect

Block W: 12.00, Block H: 12.00
Dimension 1: 8, Dimension 2: 8
Tip: Set in quilt layout for full effect

Basic Pieced Block Drawing

These exercises show the basics of drawing pieced blocks with EasyDraw™. Some blocks will be very familiar. Others may never make it into your quilts, but were chosen to teach particular skills and tools in EasyDraw™. Go into the exercises with an eagerness to learn and great secrets of EQ drawing will be revealed to you!

Students often ask "what's *your* secret for drawing blocks in EQ?" My answer: …I play a lot! I don't think of it as practice. That sounds much too boring. Instead, I enjoy challenging myself to draw complex blocks, and also play the game of "I wonder what would happen if I drew it like this?" So now you know. Now, let's draw some blocks!

Back to the Drawing Board 56
Drawing a Log Cabin Block 61
Drawing a Sawtooth Star Block 63
Drawing a Sketchbook Full of Baskets 65
Drawing a Simple Foundation Pieced House ... 76
Drawing a Drunkard's Path Block 79
Create a Four-Patch Drunkard's Path Block 81
Drawing a Double Irish Chain Block 84
Drawing a Tree of Life Block 86

Chapter 2

Chapter 2: Basic Pieced Block Drawing

Back to the Drawing Board
What's that Grid?

What is the relationship between the block size and the snap to grid points? How do you decide which numbers to use for the snap points? How can the graph paper divisions help? What's the difference between a nine-patch block and a five-patch block? In this section, we'll begin to get some answers to those questions.

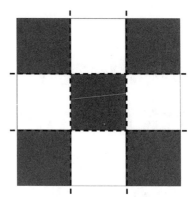

A simple Nine-Patch block

Most traditional pieced blocks can be drafted on a square grid. You have probably heard blocks referred to as "nine-patch" or "five-patch" blocks and you will see some of them as categories in EQ6's Block Library. This is not the same as the grid needed to draw the block; instead it indicates the larger units by which the block can be divided. Many times these are also the units you would stitch together first when piecing the block.

Visualize a grid of squares superimposed over the block. ***This virtual grid is the key to setting up the drawing board in EasyDraw™ for most pieced blocks.*** Once you figure out the virtual grid of a block, set the snap to grid points to that number or a multiple of that number. For example, if a block has a 3 x 3 virtual grid, set the snap to grid points at 3 x 3, 6 x 6, 12 x 12, 24 x 24 or 48 x 48. Because the number 24 is divisible by so many numbers, it's always a good place to start when you are not sure.

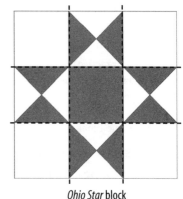

Ohio Star block

Take a look at these illustrations of three nine-patch blocks. All three are in the nine-patch category even though their subdivisions make them very different blocks. The simple *Nine Patch* block has a very obvious 3 x 3 grid. The familiar *Ohio Star* also has a 3 x 3 grid and even its triangular star points can easily be drawn on the same grid. Both the *Nine Patch* block and the *Ohio Star* snap to grid points can be set at any multiple of 3.

Now look at the third example, called *Beggar's* Block or *Homespun*. It's in the nine-patch category, but each of the nine patches can be further divided into a smaller 3 x 3 grid. It therefore has a virtual grid of 9 x 9. For this block you would need to use 9 for its snap to grid points or a multiple of 9. Setting the snap to grid points at 18 x 18 or 36 x 36 would work equally well.

Beggar's Block

Chapter 2: Basic Pieced Block Drawing

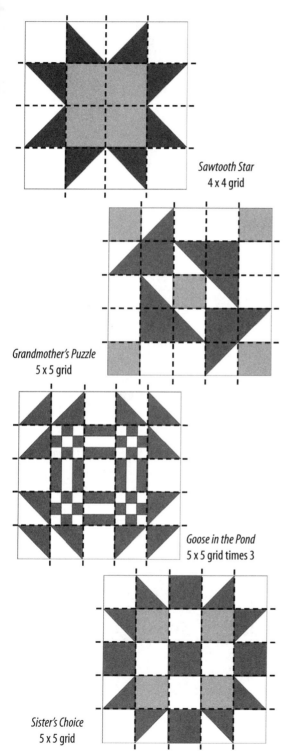

Sawtooth Star
4 x 4 grid

Grandmother's Puzzle
5 x 5 grid

Goose in the Pond
5 x 5 grid times 3

Sister's Choice
5 x 5 grid

Of course, there are pieced blocks that cannot be divided as easily as a *Nine Patch* or *Ohio Star* into a square grid. Blocks like the *LeMoyne Star* or other blocks based on a circular grid can be done in Pieced PatchDraw or Easy Draw™. We will try more blocks like those in the last chapter of this book.

Figuring out the virtual grid for some blocks is easy, but for other blocks it becomes a guessing game! I have come up with a list of seven things that will help you identify a block's virtual grid. Let's look at a few blocks from the Block Library as we go through my list.

1) Look for a Similar Block

Take a look at the *Sawtooth Star* block. See how it can be divided into a 4 x 4 virtual grid? There are many variations of this simple block and most of them can be drawn with the snap to grid points set at 24 x 24. When you are trying to figure out the snap to grid points for a new block, *look for a similar block* in the Block Library.

2) Check the Unit Classification

When you are looking through the library for a similar block, *take note of the block's category or unit classification*. For example, this *Grandmother's Puzzle* block is listed under Five Patch; that's an obvious indication of its virtual grid!

3) Subdivide the Units

Sometimes a block's unit classification can confuse you. Look at the block closely and *check to see if the units are subdivided* into smaller patches. You will need to take these smaller patches into account when you set up your drawing board. This *Goose in the Pond* block is also listed under Five Patch, but notice it has smaller 3 x 3 subunits. You will need to set your snap to grid points at 15 x 15 so that you can draw the smaller patches.

4) Look for an Obvious Grid

Some blocks make guessing the virtual grid easy. *Look to see if all the patches fit within an obvious grid.* *Sister's Choice* is a good example of this. It has a very noticeable 5 x 5 virtual grid.

Companion Book Three

Chapter 2: Basic Pieced Block Drawing

5) Find a Popular Size
A traditional *Bear's Paw* block is usually sewn as a 14" block and it's based on a 7 x 7 virtual grid. If you can find a block pattern in a book or magazine, *the size of the block is a good indication of its virtual grid.*

6) Virtually Divide Large Patches
Blocks with large patches can sometimes be tricky when you are trying to figure out their virtual grid. *Virtually divide the larger patches* into smaller squares or triangles and you can make a good guess. The large patches of the *Square within a Square* block can be divided into a 4 x 4 grid.

7) Count the Rows
The easiest way to figure out the grid for traditional *Log Cabin* type blocks or *Pineapples* is to *count the "logs" or rows of strips*. Most of time there is a larger patch in the center of the block. Virtually divide the center as if it were made up of strips as well. This *Log Cabin* block is based on an 8 x 8 grid.

We've only looked at a few blocks and discovered their virtual grids. Challenge yourself by looking at other pieced blocks from the Block Library and see if you can figure out their virtual grids. It will help you in the future when you want to edit a block or when you want to draw a block from scratch.

Block Size and Snap Points
Using EasyDraw™ to draw a pieced block is much like working with a sheet of graph paper, a pencil, and a ruler. In EQ6 the drawing board is our paper, the mouse is our pencil and the rulers are available right there on the screen. However, EasyDraw™ provides us with other special tools and features to make drawing blocks much easier than pencil and paper! You can draw blocks from scratch. You can edit blocks from the Block Library to make endless variations. You can draw a block in one size and then print the block, templates or foundation patterns any size you might need for your quilt.

Previously we talked a lot about virtual grids and how that relates to snap to grid points. But how does that help us set up our drawing board? How does that help you choose a block size right for rotary cutting the fabrics and piecing together your block?

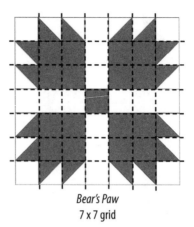

Bear's Paw
7 x 7 grid

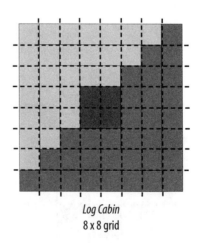

Square within a Square
4 x 4 grid

Log Cabin
8 x 8 grid

Chapter 2: Basic Pieced Block Drawing

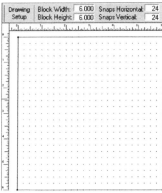

Block Size when Editing a Block

If you are editing an already existing block, the work is mostly done for you. Since EQ6 remembers the original block size and snap to grid points, you may not need to change any of the settings. Edit the block to the worktable and start drawing! You are not locked into using the remembered block size, however. You can change this if you like, but keep the block size a multiple of (or a division of) the snap to grid points.

Block Size when Drawing from Scratch

Example 1: Suppose you want to design a 6.00" square *Log Cabin* block and want 3/4" (0.75") logs. Multiply the block size by 4 so that your snap to grid points will be spaced at 1/4" increments. Since 6 x 4 = 24, set the snap to grid points at 24 x 24.

First, decide on your block size. Enter the block width and height on the Precision Bar (see page 10 for information about the Precision Bar). To set the snap to grid points, enter numbers identical to the block size numbers or a multiple of the block size.

To make the snap to grid points coincide with your ruler increments, multiply the block size by 2, 4, or 8.

- Multiply x 2 to place snap to grid points every 1/2".
- Multiply x 4 to place snap to grid points every 1/4".
- Multiply x 8 to place snap to grid points every 1/8".

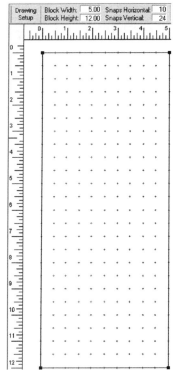

Example 2: Suppose you want to draw a rectangular sashing block that is 5.00" x 12.00". If you only need 1/2" increments to draw your block, multiply 5 x 2 to get the horizontal snap to grid points, and 12 x 2 to get the vertical snap to grid points. Set the snap to grid points at 10 x 24.

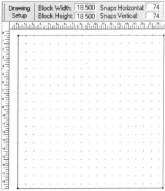

Example 3: What if you want to design an 18.50" square block? The same formula applies. So if you need 1/4" increments: 18.50 x 4 = 74. If you need 1/8" increments: 18.50 x 8 = 148.

Companion Book Three **59**

Graph Paper Divisions

I almost always use graph paper divisions when I draw a pieced block. It's much easier to draw a block from scratch if I have a visual aid to help me know where the snap to grid points are located. Usually I have the graph paper divisions match my block size, making each division represent 1". If the block's size is large you may not want that many lines on the drawing board. In that case you can make the graph paper divisions half or a quarter of the block size, making the divisions represent every two or four inches.

Graph paper divisions can only be entered in whole numbers, so if the block size is a fractional number (e.g. 4.75", 10.50" 6.25, etc.), *multiply the block size by 2 until you no longer have a fraction* for your graph paper divisions.

Perhaps you just need a visual aid to help you locate the center of an odd-sized block, set the graph paper divisions to 2 x 2. Sometimes the graph paper may not be helpful at all; in that case you can turn the visibility off.

Remember that even if you draw your block a particular size you are not limited to using only that size! It may be easier to draw the block a particular size, but you can print the block, templates, foundation patterns and rotary cutting directions for any size you may need. A word of caution: If you want to rotary cut your patches, keep your block a "ruler-friendly" size so that you can rotary cut easily.

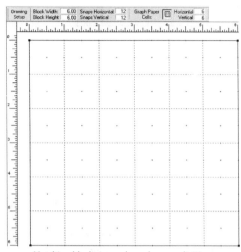

Matching block size and graph paper divisions

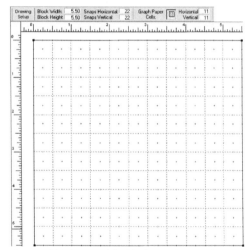

Fractional block size and double the graph paper divisions

Chapter 2: Basic Pieced Block Drawing

Drawing a Log Cabin Block

Most quilters have stitched a *Log Cabin* block. However, drawing this block can be tricky if you don't know how to set up the drawing board. Let's learn to use EQ6's helpful EasyDraw™ features to create this favorite block.

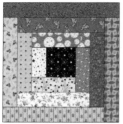

Example of a *Log Cabin* Block
(Page 23 shows the settings for drawing this same block using Pieced Patchdraw)

1   Click **WORKTABLE > Work on Block** on the top menu bar.

2   Click **BLOCK > New Block > EasyDraw Block** on the top menu bar.

Step 2

3   On the Precision Bar, enter these values pressing your keyboard TAB key after each:

Step 3

- Block Width = **8.00**
- Block Height = **8.00**
- Snaps Horizontal = **32**
- Snaps Vertical = **32**
- Graph Paper visibility is toggled **ON**
- Cells Horizontal = **8**
- Cells Vertical = **8**

4   If the rulers are not showing on the worktable, click **VIEW > Block Rulers** on the top menu bar. Like real graph paper, the EQ6 graph paper lines are a visual aid to help you draw. Setting the graph paper divisions to match your block size will make drawing much easier.

Our *Log Cabin* block is 8". So our graph paper divisions each represent 1". Following the graph paper, we know that our "logs" will be 1" wide. I multiplied my block size by 4 to get the number for the snap points. This way I know that there are four snap points per inch or graph paper division. It takes a lot of guesswork out of knowing where my lines will snap. It also means that my snap points correspond to the ruler markings.

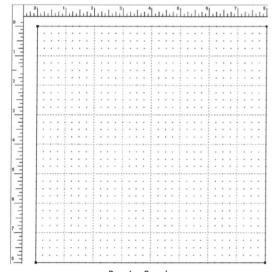

Drawing Board

Step 5
Line

5   Click the **Line** tool.

Companion Book Three   **61**

Chapter 2: Basic Pieced Block Drawing

6. In PatchDraw, you clicked and released to draw the line. Here in EasyDraw™, you need to **click and hold** as you draw a *horizontal line* from left to right beginning 1" down from the top. Release the mouse. Note how the graph paper lines show exactly where you need to draw!

> **Easy Draw™ Rule**
> All lines must connect with each other or to the edges of the block. See pages 222-230 of *EQ6 User Manual* for basic information.

7. Click and hold as you draw a *vertical line* to the bottom of the block beginning at the first drawn line and 1" from the right side of the block.

8. Draw a *horizontal line* from right to left beginning at the second drawn line and 1" from the bottom of the block.

9. Draw a *vertical line* beginning at the third drawn line and 1" from the left side of the block and ending at the first drawn line.

10. Continuing in a clockwise direction, draw *eight more lines* beginning each new line at the previously-drawn line and spacing them 1" apart. When your drawing is complete you will have a 2" square in the center of the block.

11. Click the **Add to Sketchbook** button to save your block. If any of your lines disappeared, then you need to redraw them making sure they connect with other lines or with the edges of the block.

Try the variations pictured below. All three are the same block with a few additions or subtractions.

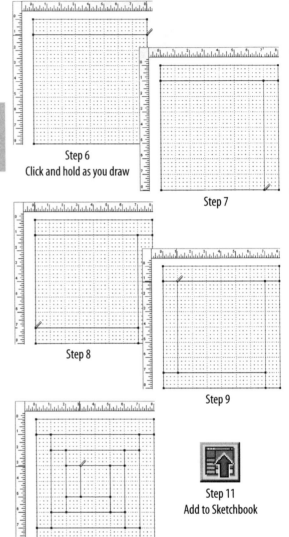

Step 6
Click and hold as you draw

Step 7

Step 8

Step 9

Step 10

Step 11
Add to Sketchbook

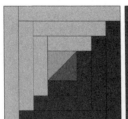

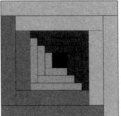

Variations of the *Log Cabin* Block

Drawing a Log Cabin Block

62 EQ6 Pieced Drawing

Chapter 2: Basic Pieced Block Drawing

Example of *Sawtooth Star* Block

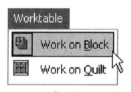

Step 1

Step 2

Step 3

Step 4
Line

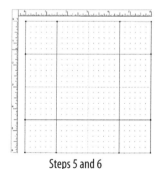

Steps 5 and 6

Drawing a Sawtooth Star Block

Here is a very popular block (also called *Variable Star*) that is easy to draw and fun to play with. Although you'll find it in the EQ6 Block Library, take the time to learn to draw it. The variations you can make with this block are almost endless.

1   Click **WORKTABLE > Work on Block**.

2   Click **BLOCK > New Block > EasyDraw Block**.

3   On the Precision Bar, enter these values pressing your keyboard TAB key after each:

- Block Width = **6.00**
- Block Height = **6.00**
- Snaps Horizontal = **24**
- Snaps Vertical = **24**
- Graph Paper visibility is toggled **ON**
- Cells Horizontal = **4**
- Cells Vertical = **4**

The *Sawtooth Star* block is drawn on a 4 x 4 grid. This is the reason the graph paper divisions were set at 4 x 4. To make sure that block size, snaps and graph paper work together, I use 24 for the snap points as it can be divided evenly by 4.

4   Click the **Line** tool.

5   Draw *two horizontal lines* across the block, one line at 1.5" and one line at 4.5".

6   Draw *two vertical lines* from the top to the bottom of the block, one at 1.5" and one at 4.5".

Companion Book Three   **63**

Chapter 2: Basic Pieced Block Drawing

7. On both sides of the block and on the top and bottom of the block, draw *two 45 degree diagonal lines* between the drawn lines, creating a flying geese unit on all sides.

8. Click the **Add to Sketchbook** button to save your block.

Try these variations of the *Sawtooth Star*.

Hint: Change the graph paper lines to 8 x 8 divisions to make the job easier!

Step 7

Step 8
Add to Sketchbook

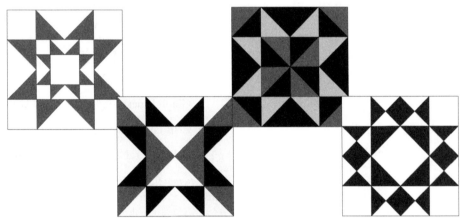

Variations of the *Sawtooth Star* Block

Chapter 2: Basic Pieced Block Drawing

Example of *Basket* Block

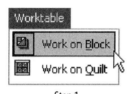

Step 1

Step 2

Step 3

Step 4
Line

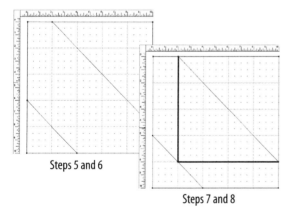

Steps 5 and 6

Steps 7 and 8

Drawing a Sketchbook Full of Baskets

Basket blocks are a fantastic excuse to practice drawing on-point blocks. We'll begin by drawing a simple on-point basket on a 5 x 5 grid. But we won't stop there. By the time you finish this exercise you will have a Sketchbook full of basket blocks. So make sure you begin a new project file for this exercise!

Basket #1

1   Click **WORKTABLE > Work on Block**.

2   Click **BLOCK > New Block > EasyDraw Block**.

3   On the Precision Bar, enter these values pressing your keyboard TAB key after each:

  - Block Width = **10.00**
  - Block Height = **10.00**
  - Snaps Horizontal = **20**
  - Snaps Vertical = **20**
  - Graph Paper visibility is toggled **ON**
  - Cells Horizontal = **5**
  - Cells Vertical = **5**

4   Click the **Line** tool.

5   Draw a diagonal line beginning at the 2" mark on the top edge of the block and ending at the 8" mark on the right edge of the block.

6   Draw a second diagonal line for the bottom of the basket beginning at 6" on the left side of the block and ending at 4" on the bottom of the block.

7   Draw a vertical line 2" from the left side down to the bottom of the basket.

8   Draw a horizontal line 2" from the bottom of the block over to the bottom of the basket.

Drawing Basket Blocks

Companion Book Three **65**

Chapter 2: Basic Pieced Block Drawing

9 Draw two 2" lines from the outside of the block to create half-square triangles at the base of the basket.

10 Click the **Add to Sketchbook** button.

Hint: You can use this base later for more variations, but first let's complete this basket by adding some half-square triangles on the top.

11 Draw a vertical and horizontal line 2" from the basket top and 2" from the right edge.

12 Draw two more lines to create two more squares, as illustrated.

13 Click the **Add to Sketchbook** button. This step will also be a base for another block.

14 To complete the basket, draw four diagonal lines perpendicular to the long diagonal of the basket bowl to create half-square triangles on the top of the basket.

15 Click the **Add to Sketchbook** button. You now have *Basket #1*.

> **Note**
> When you create on-point blocks, draw them so that the top of the design is in the upper-right corner. That way, when you set the blocks into an on-point quilt layout, the blocks will automatically be placed upright.

Now, let's take this basket block and create 15 more!

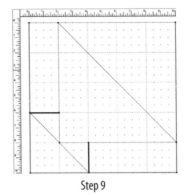
Step 9

Step 10
Add to Sketchbook

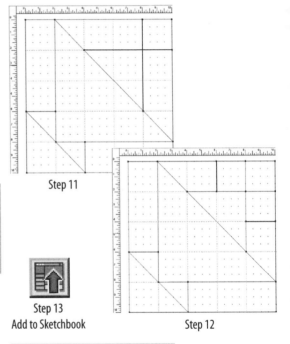
Step 11

Step 13
Add to Sketchbook

Step 12

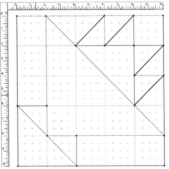
Step 14

Completed Basket #1

Chapter 2: Basic Pieced Block Drawing

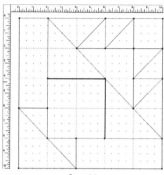

Step 16

Completed Basket #2

Basket #2

16. Start by drawing two lines to create a large square inside the bowl of the basket. Begin the lines at the center-top of the basket bowl and end them at the basket sides. Just follow the graph paper divisions!

17. Click the **Add to Sketchbook** button to save *Basket #2*.

Basket #3

18. Next draw a diagonal line parallel to the top of the basket in the square you just created.

19. Click the **Add to Sketchbook** button to save *Basket #3*.

Basket #4

20. On either side of the large square, follow the graph paper divisions and draw four lines to create smaller squares. This also creates a row of triangles along the top of basket bowl.

21. Click the **Add to Sketchbook** button to save *Basket #4*.

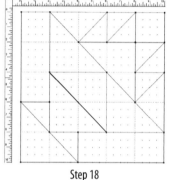

Step 18

Completed Basket #3

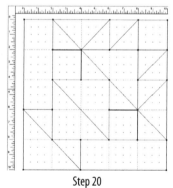

Step 20

Completed Basket #4

Companion Book Three **67**

Chapter 2: Basic Pieced Block Drawing

Basket #5

22 Draw two diagonal lines within the smaller squares created in step 20 to create half-square triangles.

23 Click the **Add to Sketchbook** button to save *Basket #5*.

Basket #6

24 Draw a square in the larger triangle at the top of the basket. Draw a diagonal line parallel to the top of the basket to create another half-square triangle.

25 Click the **Add to Sketchbook** button to save *Basket #6*. By the way, this particular basket is named *Grape Basket*.

Basket #7

26 Click the **View Sketchbook button > Blocks section > click on the basket from step 23** (*Basket #5*).

27 Click **Edit** button to place this basket block on the drawing board.

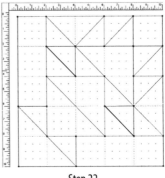

Step 22   Completed Basket #5

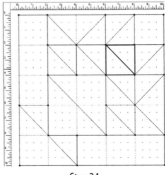

Step 24   Completed Basket #6

Step 26
View Sketchbook

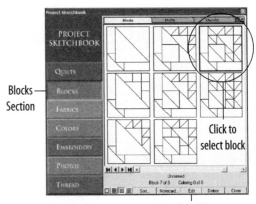

Step 27

Drawing Basket Blocks

68 EQ6 Pieced Drawing

Chapter 2: Basic Pieced Block Drawing

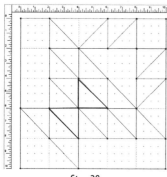

Step 28

Completed Basket #7

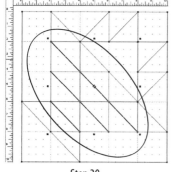

Step 30
Select lines to delete

Step 30
Pick

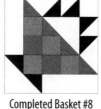

Completed Basket #8

28 Follow the graph paper divisions and draw lines to create half-square triangles in the large triangles of the basket bowl.

29 Click the **Add to Sketchbook** button to save *Basket #7*.

Basket #8

How about squares in the basket bowl? Let's erase some lines.

30 Click the **Pick tool > hold down your keyboard SHIFT key as you click each diagonal line parallel to the top of the basket**, to select them. (That's six clicks.)

> **Note**
> If you select the wrong line, simply SHIFT + click the line again to deselect it.

31 Press your keyboard **DELETE** key to delete these selected lines.

32 Click the **Add to Sketchbook** button to save *Basket #8*.

Basket #9

Let's take a different track now and change the top part of our basket block.

33 Click the **View Sketchbook button > Blocks section > click on the base basket saved in step 13**.

34 Click the **Edit** button to place this basket block on the drawing board.

Step 32
Add to Sketchbook

Step 33
View Sketchbook

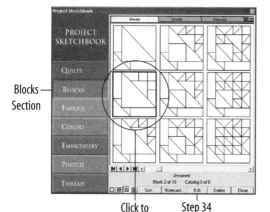

Blocks Section

Click to select block   Step 34

Drawing Basket Blocks

Companion Book Three   **69**

Chapter 2: Basic Pieced Block Drawing

35. Click the **Line** tool.

36. Draw two lines to create an additional square along both the top and right sides of the block.

37. Draw diagonal lines parallel to the top of the basket to create half-square triangles in all the squares along the basket top.

38. Click the **Add to Sketchbook** button to save *Basket #9*.

Basket #10

39. In the large triangle at the top of the basket block, draw one more half-square triangle.

40. Click the **Add to Sketchbook** button to save *Basket #10*.

Step 35
Line

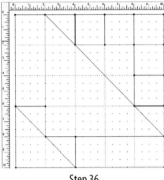

Step 36

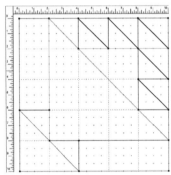

Step 37   Completed Basket #9

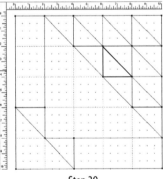

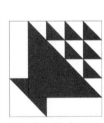

Step 39   Completed Basket #10

Chapter 2: Basic Pieced Block Drawing

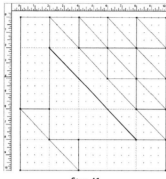
Step 41

Basket #11

41 Draw a long diagonal line parallel to the top of the basket bowl.

42 Draw lines to create a row of triangles along the top of the basket bowl.

43 Click the **Add to Sketchbook** button to save *Basket #11*.

Notice with this block we created a smaller basket bowl!

Basket #12

44 Click the **Pick tool > hold down your keyboard SHIFT key as you click to select lines to be deleted** so that you will create a mirror image triangle opposite the basket bowl.

45 Press your keyboard **DELETE** key.

46 Click the **Add to Sketchbook** button to save *Basket #12*.

Now that you have a smaller basket base, do you think you can create another series of baskets? I'll show you four more ideas for baskets. Use these as inspiration to create more of your own unique blocks.

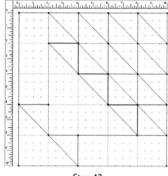
Step 42

Step 44
Pick

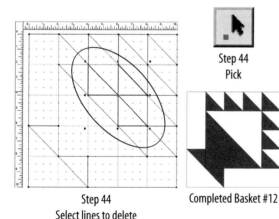
Step 44
Select lines to delete

Completed Basket #11

Completed Basket #12

Drawing Basket Blocks

Companion Book Three   **71**

Chapter 2: Basic Pieced Block Drawing

Basket #13

47 Click the **View Sketchbook button > Blocks section > click base basket saved in step 10**.

48 Click the **Edit** button to place this basket block on the drawing board.

Let's draw a *Sawtooth Star* block on our basket block. There are several ways to do this. But we'll draw so the star block appears to hang over the top of the basket.

Look at the graph paper divisions. Find the 4 x 4 grid in the top-right corner of the block. This is where we will draw the *Sawtooth Star*.

49 Click the **Line** tool.

50 Begin by drawing the center square of the *Sawtooth Star* (a 4" square).

51 Next draw the lines that create the star points.

52 Click the **Add to Sketchbook** button to save *Basket #13*.

Step 47
View Sketchbook

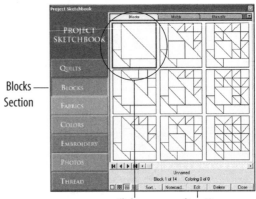

Blocks Section

Click to select block

Step 48

Step 49
Line

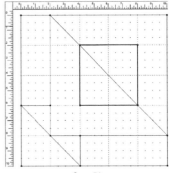

Step 50

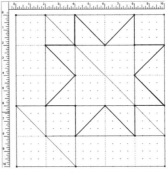

Step 51

Completed Basket #13

Chapter 2: Basic Pieced Block Drawing

Step 53
View Sketchbook

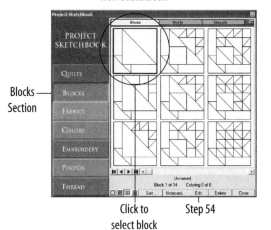

Blocks Section

Click to select block

Step 54

Step 55

Basket #14

For the last three blocks we'll create a totally new look, changing the base and even adding a handle.

53 Click the **View Sketchbook button > Blocks section > click base basket saved in step 10**.

54 Click the **Edit** button to place this basket block on the drawing board.

55 On the Precision Bar, change the *Graph Paper Cells* to **10 x 10**. Press your keyboard **ENTER** key to make the change.

56 Click the **Line** tool.

57 At the bottom of the basket bowl, draw a diagonal line from node to node parallel to the base.

58 Click the **Pick** tool.

59 Hold down your keyboard **SHIFT** key and click each of the two lines at the inside base of the basket bowl, to select them.

Step 56
Line

Step 58
Pick

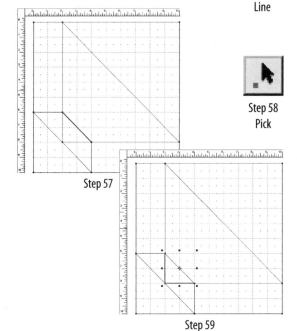

Step 57

Step 59
Select lines to delete

Drawing Basket Blocks

Companion Book Three   **73**

Chapter 2: Basic Pieced Block Drawing

60 Press your keyboard **DELETE** key to delete the selected lines.

This makes our basket look like it has a flat bottom.

61 Click the **Line** tool.

62 To draw the handle, first draw a horizontal line 1" down from the top of the block, beginning at the top of the basket and ending on the right side of the block.

63 Draw two vertical lines spaced 1" apart from the right side of the block. Begin at the horizontal line we just drew, and end at the top of the basket.

64 To complete the handle, draw another horizontal line 1" below the first one beginning at the basket top and ending at the inside of the right handle.

65 Click the **Add to Sketchbook** button to save *Basket #14*.

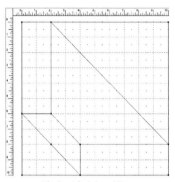
Block with deleted lines

Step 61
Line

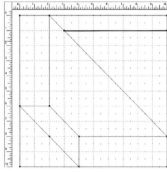
Step 62

Step 63

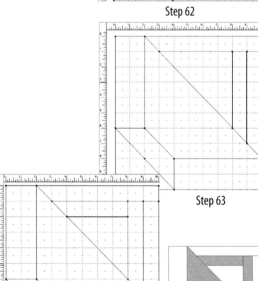
Step 64   Completed Basket #14

Chapter 2: Basic Pieced Block Drawing

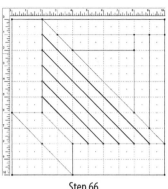

Step 66

Completed Basket #15

Step 68

Step 69
Line

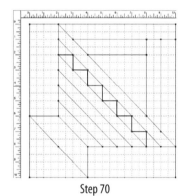

Step 70

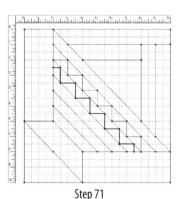

Step 71

Completed Basket #16

Basket #15

How about some stripes on your basket?

66 To draw stripes, follow the graph paper intersections and draw five diagonal lines parallel to the basket top, beginning and ending 1" down on the sides of the basket.

67 Click the **Add to Sketchbook** button to save *Basket #15*.

Basket #16

Let's finish off our exercise by changing some *Basket #15* stripes to zig zags.

68 On the Precision bar, change the *Graph Paper Cells* to **20 x 20**. Press your keyboard **ENTER** key to make the change.

69 Click the **Line** tool.

70 Beginning in the second stripe from the top of the basket, draw horizontal and vertical lines to create a row of triangles within the stripe.

71 In the stripe just beneath the row of triangles, draw another row of triangles, but this time alternate the triangles so that they create a zigzag design across the basket. Begin and end this row of triangles with a short 1/2" line to the basket edge, as shown.

72 Click the **Add to Sketchbook** button to save *Basket #16!*

I hope you have had fun with these baskets—I sure did! Just by changing the line directions and the graph paper divisions we created 16 different baskets, and I'm guessing you can already think of even more variations.

These basket blocks are perfect to use in a theme quilt, or as a quilt guild block exchange. Of course you realize this is not the only basket block you can edit like this. And if you don't like baskets, go ahead and try another block and see where it leads you.

Companion Book Three

Chapter 2: Basic Pieced Block Drawing

Drawing a Simple Foundation Pieced House Block

I consider a simple foundation block as one having only horizontal and vertical lines, and no angle sharper than 45 degrees. These blocks may have more than one unit or section. But the seam lines easily follow the graph paper divisions. In the simple little house we'll build there are no odd angles to draw or sew.

Example of *Foundation Pieced House* Block

1   Click **WORKTABLE > Work on Block**.

2   Click **BLOCK > New Block > EasyDraw Block**.

3   On the Precision Bar, enter these values pressing your keyboard TAB key after each:

- Block Width = **4.00**
- Block Height = **5.00**
- Snaps Horizontal = **16**
- Snaps Vertical = **20**
- Graph Paper visibility is toggled **ON**
- Cells Horizontal = **16**
- Cells Vertical = **20**

Step 1

Step 2

Step 3

Notice that I matched my graph paper divisions to the snap to grid points. This will make it easier to draw the smaller parts of our house. So for this block, each graph paper division is equal to 1/4" (0.25).

When it comes to foundation block drawing, think backwards—work backwards from the way you would stitch the block together. When you *sew* a foundation pieced block you join smaller pieces to form larger units. Then you assemble these units to form the whole block.

When you *draw* the block in EasyDraw™ you first divide the whole into smaller units. Then you break these units into still smaller sections and subsections.

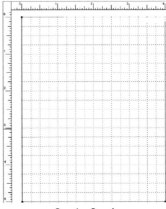

Drawing Board

Chapter 2: Basic Pieced Block Drawing

Step 4
Line

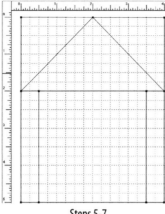
Steps 5-7

4   Click the **Line** tool.

First, let's divide the block into two sections, one for the roof and one for the main part of the house.

5   Draw a horizontal line 2" from the top of the block.

6   In the top section, draw two 45 degree lines from the sides to the top center creating the roof.

7   In the bottom section, draw two vertical lines to create the sides of the house, 1/2" in from the block outline. This also creates a roof overhang.

8   Click the **Add to Sketchbook** button to save this block.

You can use this drawing again to make variations of your house.

9   Draw a horizontal line from one side of the house to the other 1" below the roof. This will be the height of our door. Since our door is larger than our window, we will draw that first.

10   Create the door by first drawing a vertical line in the center of the block from the door height line to the bottom of the block. Then draw a second vertical line 1" to the left.

11   In the window section, draw two horizontal lines 1/2" from the top and bottom of the section. Then draw two vertical lines 1/2" from the sides to complete the window.

12   Click the **Add to Sketchbook** button.

Step 8
Add to Sketchbook

Steps 9 and 10

Step 12
Add to Sketchbook

Step 11

EQ6 is working in the background, taking care of the business of making your block into a foundation pattern. However, we need to do our part to help EQ6 do its job successfully. I've drawn and stitched many foundation pieced blocks over the years, and have discovered four basic principles we need to remember when drawing foundation pieced blocks. These hold true whether drawing on paper or drawing and printing out the pattern from EQ6. Our goal is to end up with a block we can successfully foundation piece, right?

Drawing a Simple House Block

Companion Book Three   **77**

Chapter 2: Basic Pieced Block Drawing

Four Principles for Drawing Foundations

First, draw with *straight lines*. Foundation piecing is based on straight lines. It's those easy-to-stitch straight lines that make foundation piecing so popular!

Second, work from *large to small*. Draw larger units first. Then break down each unit separately into smaller patches.

Third, *simplify*. Whether your foundation block is simple or complex you must try to *simplify the design* so that it can be stitched together with straight seams.

Fourth, *avoid creating inside corners*. EQ6 cannot create a foundation pattern when there are inside corners (also known as set-in seams or y-seams). And besides, they're difficult to stitch on the sewing machine. Avoiding inside corners takes practice. Most of the time we overlook them until we go to print our foundation pattern. We'll talk more about this in a later exercise when we draw a foundation pieced block that has a lot more pieces and odd angles.

So remember these four things whenever you draw a foundation pieced block:

- Straight lines
- Large to small
- Simplify
- Avoid inside corners

Now that we have that out of the way, you might want to try these variations of the house block. Feel free to create your own house!

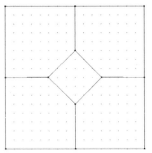

This block has an inside corner

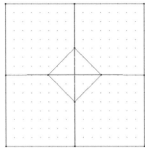

Adding two lines makes this block foundation piecable

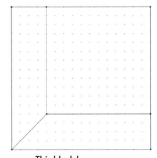

This block has a y-seam

Removing the y-seam creates an easier piecing

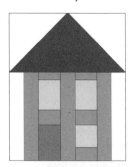
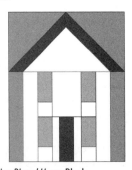

Variations of the *Foundation Pieced House* Block

Drawing a Drunkard's Path Block

Drawing arcs is an important addition to your EQ6 drawing skills. The *Drunkard's Path* block offers an excellent chance to practice drawing arcs. Hundreds of blocks are based on this simple arc design. This particular version is good practice for cloning and flipping too!

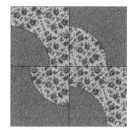

Example of *Drunkard's Path* Block

1   Click **WORKTABLE > Work on Block**.

2   Click **BLOCK > New Block > EasyDraw Block**.

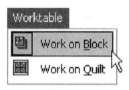

Step 1

3   On the Precision Bar, enter these values pressing your keyboard TAB key after each:

- Block Width = **6.00**

Step 2

- Block Height = **6.00**
- Snaps Horizontal = **24**
- Snaps Vertical = **24**

Step 3

- Graph Paper visibility is toggled **ON**
- Cells Horizontal = **6**
- Cells Vertical = **6**

4   Click the **Line** tool.

5   Draw a horizontal and vertical line to divide the block into a four patch.

6   Click the **Arc** tool.

Step 4
Line

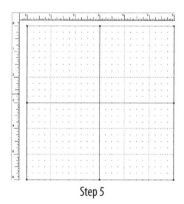

Step 5

Step 6
Arc

Companion Book Three   **79**

Chapter 2: Basic Pieced Block Drawing

7. In the top-left square, draw a 2" right-facing arc as shown. Begin the arc on the left side 1" down from the top of the square. End it 2" from the left side of the square. *Repeat* in the top-right and lower-right squares.

> **Note**
> To change the arc's direction as you're drawing, press your keyboard SPACEBAR before releasing the mouse button.

8. In the lower-left square, draw the same size arc upside down in the corner towards the center of the square (press the **SPACEBAR** to flip the direction of the arc). It will be a mirror image of the arc in top-right square.

9. Click the **Add to Sketchbook** button to save this block.

> **Note**
> This asymmetrical *Drunkard's Path* block is a lot of fun to play with in a quilt layout. Color the block with fabrics. Place it in a 4 x 4 horizontal quilt layout. Use the Symmetry tool on the Quilt worktable and see what happens! (See page 164 of the *EQ6 User Manual* for details on using this cool tool.)

Below are some other *Drunkard's Path* type blocks you can try.

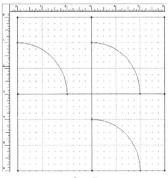

Step 7

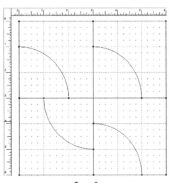

Step 8

Step 9
Add to Sketchbook

Variations of the Drunkard's Path Block

Chapter 2: Basic Pieced Block Drawing

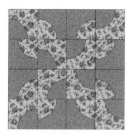

Example of *Four-Patch Drunkard's Path* Block

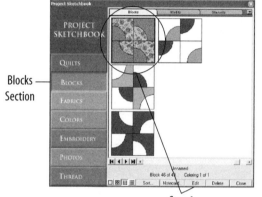

Blocks Section

Step 1

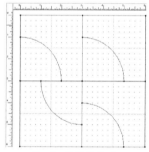

Drunkard's Path Block

Step 2

Step 3
Pick

Symmetry Box

Create a Four-Patch Drunkard's Path Block

To do this exercise you need to first complete the "Drawing a Drunkard's Path Block" lesson (see page 79). This shows you how to draw and rotate arcs to get the traditional "path."

1. Retrieve the **Drunkard's Path** block you drew from the exercise on page 79 and edit it to the worktable. To do so, click the **View Sketchbook button > Blocks section > click the *Drunkard's Path* block > click the Edit button**. (If you have not done the *Drunkard's Path* exercise, do so now.)

2. On the Precision Bar, enter these values pressing your keyboard TAB key after each:

   - Block Width = **6.00**
   - Block Height = **6.00**
   - Snaps Horizontal = **24**
   - Snaps Vertical = **24**
   - Graph Paper visibility is toggled **ON**
   - Cells Horizontal = **4**
   - Cells Vertical = **4**

3. On the **Pick** tool, click the **small red square.** This brings up the Symmetry box.

Drawing a Drunkard's Path Block

Companion Book Three   **81**

Chapter 2: Basic Pieced Block Drawing

4. Click **EDIT > Select All** on the top menu bar. (Keyboard shortcut: **CTRL+A**) This selects all lines on the block.

> **Note**
> Patches will stay selected unless you click somewhere else on the drawing board, which de-selects the patches.

5. **Right-click** on the block > choose **Resize** from the menu that pops up > enter **50** in both the horizontal and vertical boxes > click **OK**.

Step 4

> **Note**
> When the Resize box opens, the horizontal size is already highlighted, so you can type the new number right into the number box. Press the keyboard TAB key twice and it will take you to the vertical box.

6. Move your cursor to the center of the selected patches so that it turns into a 4-headed arrow. **Click and drag** the still-selected and resized patches to the upper-left quadrant of the block, matching the center line of the patches with the lines of the graph paper, taking care to *make sure they snap into place*.

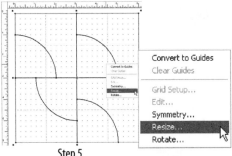
Step 5

> **Notes**
> - When moving selected patches, move them just a hair away from the target so that you can visually see them snap into place.
>
> - When moving a group of selected patches, be sure to move your cursor to the center of the selection so the cursor turns into a 4-headed arrow. Then click and drag the selection.
>
> - If you accidentally click away from the patches, so they are no longer selected, try choosing EDIT > Undo (CTRL+Z) to take you back to the point where your patches are still selected. If this does not work, you may need to retrieve the block again from the Sketchbook and start over.

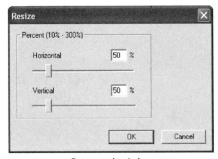
Enter number in box

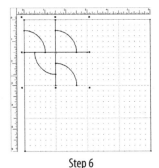
Step 6
Drag to upper-left quadrant

Chapter 2: Basic Pieced Block Drawing

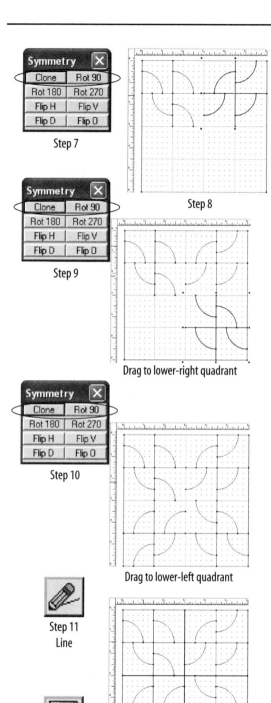

Step 7

Step 8

Step 9

Drag to lower-right quadrant

Step 10

Drag to lower-left quadrant

Step 11 Line

Step 13 Add to Sketchbook

Step 12

7. While the patches are still selected, **click Clone > then click Rot 90** (rotate 90 degrees).

> **Note**
> When cloning and rotating 90 degrees in succession (as we did for this block), remember to repeat the process while the patches are still selected.

8. Drag the still-selected clone to the upper-right quadrant, *making sure it snaps into place*.

9. Click **Clone again > click Rot 90 > drag the clone to the lower-right quadrant**.

10. Click **Clone again > click Rot 90 > drag the clone to the lower-left quadrant**.

11. Click the **Line** tool.

12. Following the graph paper lines, draw a horizontal and a vertical line in the center of the block, dividing it into a four patch.

13. Click the **Add to Sketchbook** button to save the block.

If you drew the variations from the previous *Drunkard's Path* exercise, try making them into a four-patch block too. You can come up with some interesting new blocks!

Variations of *Four-Patch Drunkard's Path* Block

Drawing a Drunkard's Path Block

Companion Book Three   **83**

Chapter 2: Basic Pieced Block Drawing

Drawing a Double Irish Chain Block

Made up of only square patches, you can make quick work of drawing this block by using the Grid tool.

1. Click **WORKTABLE > Work on Block**.

2. Click **BLOCK > New Block > EasyDraw Block**.

3. On the Precision Bar, enter these values pressing your keyboard TAB key after each:

   - Block Width = **10.00**
   - Block Height = **10.00**
   - Snaps Horizontal = **20**
   - Snaps Vertical = **20**
   - Graph Paper visibility is toggled **ON**
   - Cells Horizontal = **10**
   - Cells Vertical = **10**

4. Click the **Line** tool.

5. Following the graph paper lines, draw a horizontal and a vertical line in the center of the block, dividing it into a four patch.

6. On the **Grid** tool, click the **small red square** on the button. This brings up the Grid Setup box.

7. In the Grid Setup box, click the arrow buttons to change the number to **5** for both *Columns* and *Rows*.

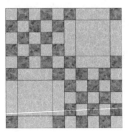

Example of *Double Irish Chain* Block

Step 1

Step 2

Step 3

Step 4
Line

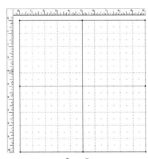

Step 5

Step 6
Grid

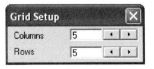

Step 7
Grid Setup Box

84   EQ6 Pieced Drawing

Chapter 2: Basic Pieced Block Drawing

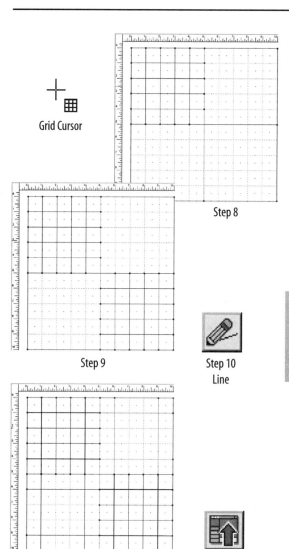

Grid Cursor

Step 8

Step 9

Step 10 Line

Step 11

Step 12 Add to Sketchbook

Notice that the cursor has changed to a crosshair with a grid.

8   Point the cursor at the upper-left corner of the block, then **click** and **drag diagonally** to the center point of the block and release the mouse. A 5 x 5 grid is now placed in the upper-left quadrant of the block.

9   Still using the **Grid** tool, point the cursor at the exact center of the block, then **click** and **drag diagonally** to the bottom-right corner of the block. A 5 x 5 grid is now placed in the lower-right quadrant of the block.

You may need to click on the refresh tool after drawing the grids to make them more visible.

> **Note**
> When you place your mouse cursor cross hair on the block, you need to drag the cursor diagonally. If you make a mistake, use CTRL+Z to undo your drawing immediately, or simply click EDIT > Undo.

10 Click the **Line** tool.

11 In each of the remaining two quadrants of the block, draw four lines (two horizontal and two vertical) 1" away from the grids and from the edge of the block (see illustration). This creates a 3" framed square in these remaining quadrants and completes the *Double Irish Chain* block.

12 Click the **Add to Sketchbook** button to save your block.

Try these variations of the *Double Irish Chain*.

Variations of *Double Irish Chain* Block

Companion Book Three   **85**

Chapter 2: Basic Pieced Block Drawing

Drawing a Tree of Life Block

To draw this block you'll use many skills you learned earlier in this chapter. You'll also find a handy use for the Xings tool. Don't know what the Xings tool is? Let's find out!

Example of *Tree of Life* Block

1   Click **WORKTABLE > Work on Block**.

2   Click **BLOCK > New Block > EasyDraw Block**.

3   On the Precision Bar, enter these values pressing your keyboard TAB key after each:

- Block Width = **10.00**
- Block Height = **10.00**
- Snaps Horizontal = **20**
- Snaps Vertical = **20**
- Graph Paper visibility is toggled **ON**
- Cells Horizontal = **10**
- Cells Vertical = **10**

4   Click the **Line** tool.

5   Following the graph paper lines, draw a horizontal and a vertical line in the center of the block, dividing the block into a four patch.

6   Next you'll draw two diagonal lines. Draw one in the upper-left quadrant, beginning at 4" on the top edge and ending at 4" on the left edge. Draw the second diagonal in the lower-right quadrant, beginning at 6" on the bottom and ending at 6" on the right.

7   On the **Grid** tool, click the **small red square** on the button. This brings up the Grid Setup box.

8   In the Grid Setup box, click the arrow buttons to change the number to **5** for both *Columns* and *Rows*.

Next we'll use the Grid tool to create a 5 x 5 grid in the upper-left, upper-right and lower-right quadrants of the block.

Step 1

Step 2

Step 3

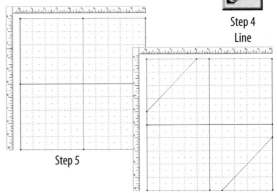

Step 4
Line

Step 5

Step 6

Step 7
Grid

Step 8

Chapter 2: Basic Pieced Block Drawing

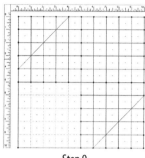

Step 9
5 x 5 grid over three quadrants

Step 10
Shape

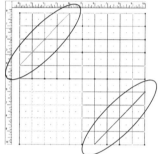

Steps 11-13
Click line to select

Click Xings

Step 14
Pick

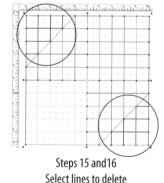

Steps 15 and 16
Select lines to delete

9 Point the cursor at the upper-left corner of the quadrant, then **click** and **drag the mouse diagonally** to the bottom-right of the quadrant to create a 5 x 5 grid. *Repeat* for the upper-right and lower-right quadrants, as illustrated. **Do not add it to the Sketchbook yet!**

10 On the **Shape** tool, click the **small red square** on the button. This brings up the Edit Line box.

11 Click on one of the diagonal lines from step 6, to select it.

12 Click on **Xings** on the Edit Line box.

13 Click the **other diagonal line > click on Xings**.

Note
Using Xings (crossings) to establish nodes only along the diagonal line makes it easier to delete parts of the grid that we created but that won't be needed in the final block. We did not want to save the block to the Sketchbook before we clicked Xings, because that would have made you do a lot more clicking to delete all those unwanted lines!

14 Click the **Pick** tool.

15 Hold down your keyboard **SHIFT** key, and click on each line that is to the left of the diagonal line in the upper-left quadrant (see illustration) to select them.

16 Still holding down **SHIFT**, click on each line to the right of the diagonal line in the lower-right quadrant.

Note
If you select a line by accident, click the line again, still holding down the SHIFT key, to deselect it.

17 Press your keyboard **DELETE** key to delete these unwanted lines.

Chapter 2: Basic Pieced Block Drawing

18. Now click the **Add to Sketchbook** button!

19. Click the **Line** tool again.

20. To create the tree top, draw diagonal lines as illustrated to create small half-square triangles. Notice there is no diagonal line drawn from the block center to the upper-right corner. These are to remain open squares.

21. To create the top of the tree trunk, draw a horizontal line at 6" and a vertical line at 4" ending at the nodes on the tree top. This creates a square in the upper-right corner of this quadrant.

22. Using the graph paper lines as your guide, draw two short lines to create a 1" square next to the square you created in the upper-right corner of this quadrant (as illustrated).

23. Click the **Add to Sketchbook** button to establish nodes.

Step 18
Add to Sketchbook

Step 19
Line

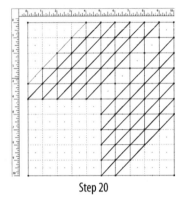
Step 20

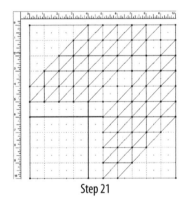
Step 21

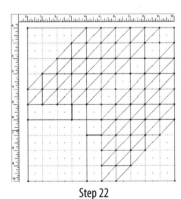
Step 22

Step 23
Add to Sketchbook

Chapter 2: Basic Pieced Block Drawing

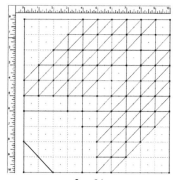
Step 24

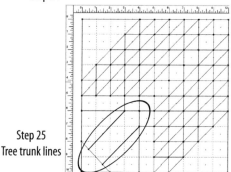
Step 25
Tree trunk lines

Step 27
Add to Sketchbook

24. Draw a diagonal line in the lower-left corner, beginning the line at 8" on the left edge and ending at 2" on the bottom edge.

25. To create the tree trunk, we'll draw two diagonal lines going from right to left this time. Begin the lines at the node on the top of the tree trunk and end them at the diagonal line you created in the left corner. These lines will be perpendicular to the corner line.

26. To complete the base of the tree, draw two short lines from the tree trunk to the block outline, as illustrated.

27. Click the **Add to Sketchbook** button to save your block.

> **Note**
> This block is most often made on a larger scale and set on-point as the center in a medallion-style quilt. Keep in mind the finished size of the half-square triangles when deciding how large to make the block. For instance, if the finished block size is 20", the half-square triangles in the tree top will be 2".

Try these *Tree of Life* block variations, or use what you have learned and create your own unique tree!

 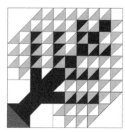

Variations of *Tree of Life* Block

Step 26

Companion Book Three

Divide & Conquer!

In this chapter we will work with a variety of blocks learning to use more advanced tools and skills in drawing with EasyDraw™. We'll practice merging, partitioning, staggering, deleting, flipping and rotating to create new blocks as well as edit existing ones. Several of the exercises will deal with arc and circular blocks in EasyDraw™.

Playing with Merged Blocks 92
Drawing Prairie Braid Strips 97
Wacky Cabins, Stars & Pineapples 101
Drawing a Winding Ways Block 104
Drawing Fan Blocks 106
Drawing a Dresden Plate Block 110
Drawing a Mariner's Compass 114
From Compass to Foundation 118
Drawing a Circle of Geese Block 122
Drawing Curved Geese Block 126
Drawing a Giant Dahlia Block 130

Chapter 3

Chapter 3: Divide and Conquer!

Playing with Merged Blocks

EQ6 has a new feature available on the BLOCK menu called Serendipity. We can take blocks already in our Sketchbook and add a preset frame, tilt them at angles or even merge them into another block. This last feature, called Merge Blocks is what we are going to play with in this exercise. We'll start with merging blocks from the library and then I'll show you how to edit blocks to create a new merge setting. I know you will see lots of other possibilities!

Step 2

1. Start a new project file for this exercise. We'll be creating a lot of new blocks, so starting with a new project file will give you lots of room!

2. First, let's get two blocks to work with from the library. Click **LIBRARIES > Block Library > EQ6 Libraries.** Under **1 Classic Pieced: Variable Stars**, select the *Sawtooth Star* and click the **Add to Sketchbook** button. Under **Nine Patch Stars** select and add *Aunt Eliza's Star* to the Sketchbook. **Close** the Block Library.

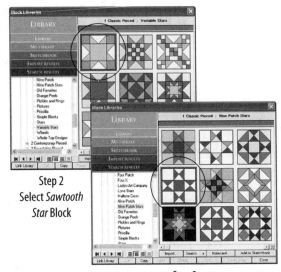

Step 2
Select *Sawtooth Star* Block

Step 2
Select *Aunt Eliza's Star* Block

3. Click the **Work on Block** button to be sure you are on the Block worktable. Click **BLOCK > Serendipity > Merge Blocks**. On the left of the Merge Blocks dialog you will see the background blocks and on the right you will see the blocks you can merge with the background blocks.

Step 3

Not all the blocks added to the Sketchbook will appear on the left as background blocks in the **Merge Blocks** dialog. EQ evaluates each block in the Sketchbook and decides if it is suitable as a background block. Only blocks that meet the following requirements will show:

- Blocks must be **EasyDraw™ blocks** created on the EasyDraw™ worktable, or blocks from the Library that have been drawn using EasyDraw™.

- The block must have at least **one parallelogram** (squares or rectangles included) that is larger than other patches.

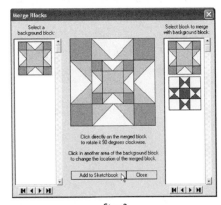

Step 3

92   EQ6 Pieced Drawing

Chapter 3: Divide and Conquer!

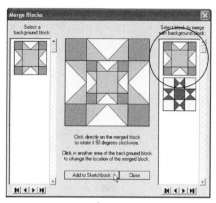
Step 4

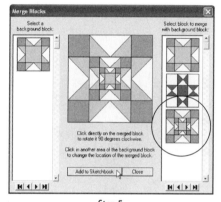
Step 5

Step 6
View Sketchbook

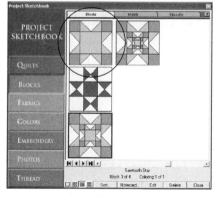
Step 6

- The **size** of the parallelogram must take up a certain amount of space in the block. For example, *Aunt Eliza's Star* has equal sized patches, so it is not suitable for a background block and does not appear on the left.

4   In the Merge Blocks dialog, select the **Sawtooth Star** on the left, and then on the right, click on the **Sawtooth Star**. At first the smaller star is added to the center patch, but you can also add it to the corner squares by clicking the corners in the block preview. For now, let's add it to the center square creating a star within a star. Click **Add to Sketchbook**. Don't close the dialog—we're going to merge it again!

5   Still using the *Sawtooth Star* as the background block, scroll down on the right side of the dialog to the last block and select it (this is the block you just added). Click **Add to Sketchbook**. Now you have a star within a star *times two!* You can repeat this a few more times if you like. **Close** the Merge Blocks dialog when you are done.

Now let's edit the *Sawtooth Star* block and make a new space to merge blocks into.

6   Click the **View Sketchbook** button to open the Sketchbook. Select the original *Sawtooth Star*, then click **Edit** to place it on the worktable.

7   If the Precision Bar is not turned on, click **VIEW > Precision Bar** to open it.

Playing with Merged Blocks

Companion Book Three   **93**

Chapter 3: Divide and Conquer!

8. On the Precision Bar, change the block size to **8.00 x 8.00**, leave snap to grid points at **16 x 16** and change the graph paper divisions to **8 x 8**.

9. Click the **Line** tool and draw a vertical line down the center square patch dividing it in half.

10. Switch to the **Pick** tool. While holding down the **SHIFT** key, select the two diagonal lines creating the right points on the star as well as the two *vertical* lines that connect these points, as illustrated. Right-click and choose **Convert to Guides** from the context menu.

This does two things. One, by deleting the lines it created a new patch to merge blocks into. And two, the guidelines will help us redraw part of the block later.

11. Click **Add to Sketchbook**.

12. Click **BLOCK > Serendipity > Merge Blocks**.

13. On the left, scroll down to the end of the background blocks and choose the new block you saved in step 11. On the right choose the **Sawtooth Star**. The *Sawtooth Star* should be in the new patch of the background block in the preview. Click **Add to Sketchbook** and then click **Close**.

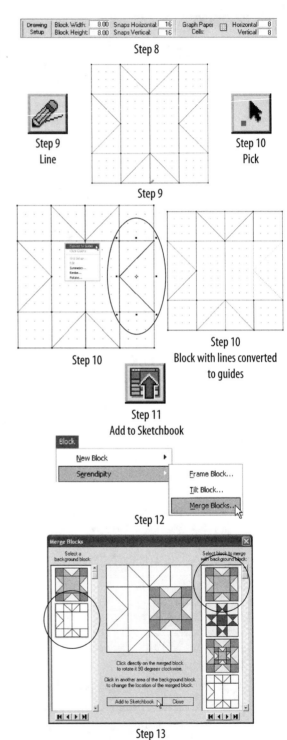

94   EQ6 Pieced Drawing

Chapter 3: Divide and Conquer!

Step 14
View Sketchbook

Step 15
Line

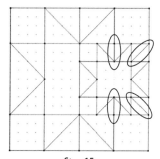
Step 15
Redraw lines of largest star

Step 16
Add to Sketchbook

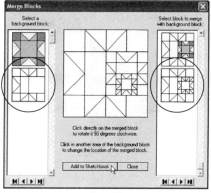
Step 17

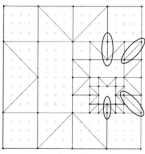
Step 18
Redraw the lines of the largest star

Step 19
Add to Sketchbook

14 Click **View Sketchbook** and retrieve the new block you just saved and place it on the worktable.

Now let's redraw some of the lines of the original star so that our new block looks like it is made up of overlapping stars.

15 Click the **Line** tool and redraw the lines of the largest star that fall outside the smaller one. This is what will make it look like the stars overlap. Now you know why we converted those lines to guides!

16 Click **Add to Sketchbook** to save the block.

At this point I recommend you color the block and name it on the Notecard. It will make it easier to spot in the Sketchbook, because we are going to merge it one more time!

17 Click **BLOCK > Serendipity > Merge Blocks**. On the left, select the block again that was saved in step 11. On the right, scroll down to the bottom and choose the block that was just added to the Sketchbook. When you look at the new block, notice that the smaller star is on the bottom in the preview. Since it's asymmetrical we can rotate it 90 degrees for a different look. Click on the block in the preview to rotate it. Continue to click until you find the best rotation. Click **Add to Sketchbook**. If you like, you can add all four rotations. Click **Close** when you are done.

18 You will need to redraw the lines of the large star again. Retrieve the newly merged block from the Sketchbook and place it on the worktable. Click the **Line** tool and redraw the lines of the largest star as before, but draw only those that would fall outside both of the smaller stars.

19 Click **Add to Sketchbook**. If you added other rotations, redraw the lines for the largest star for them as well while the guidelines are still on the drawing board. Guidelines are not saved when you exit a project file.

Playing with Merged Blocks

Companion Book Three   **95**

Chapter 3: Divide and Conquer!

IMPORTANT
Take the time to rename and color the completed merged blocks you want to keep. It's very easy to lose track when you're merging blocks! If your background block is named, the merged block will keep the same name.

You can continue to play with the *Sawtooth Star*, but you might like to edit the *Aunt Eliza's Star* too. I deleted the lines in the center of the star to create a new patch suitable for merging. The main difference is this time the blocks you add to the center will be on-point.

Did you do the Basket exercise on page 65? If you did, here is a fun idea you can try. Pick one of the baskets and draw a square on the bowl of the basket (or just use Basket #2). Merge other blocks into the square to decorate the basket with small blocks.

There are so many possibilities with merged blocks that I could not list them all. Experiment with different blocks and see what happens!

Note
Keep your merged blocks sewing-friendly! When you edit to create new patches, think ahead about how it will need to be sewn together. You may need to redraw lines or add new ones so that you can stitch the block together easily. You may also want to change the block size since merged blocks adopt the size of the background block. Change graph paper divisions to match the block dimensions to make drawing easier.

Variations of *Sawtooth Star* Block

Variations of *Aunt Eliza's Star* Block

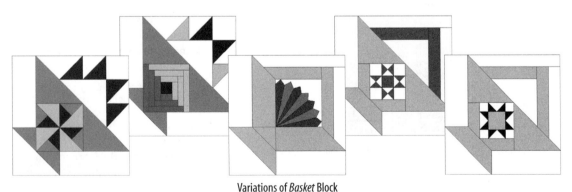

Variations of *Basket* Block

Chapter 3: Divide and Conquer!

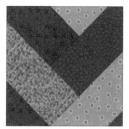

Example of *Prairie Braid Strip*

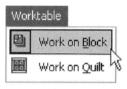

Step 1

Step 2

Step 3

Step 4
Line

Step 5

Drawing Prairie Braid Strips

I'm not sure when this string-pieced block was first named *Prairie Braid*. There is a similar block dated 1898 called *Twist and Turn* attributed to Ladies Art Company in Barbara Brackman's *Encyclopedia of Pieced Quilt Patterns* (#481). String-pieced blocks are as popular today as they were over a century ago. This block is ideal for foundation piecing and using up leftover strips of fabric.

Although this block is simple to sew, figuring out how to draw can be confusing because you need to create a block that is repeatable. In this exercise I'll show you how to create a repeating braid block as well as how to quickly transform it into a long strip.

1   Click **WORKTABLE > Work on block**.

2   Click **BLOCK > New Block > EasyDraw Block**.

3   On the Precision Bar, enter these values pressing your keyboard TAB key after each:

- Block Width = **8.00**
- Block Height = **8.00**
- Snaps Horizontal = **8**
- Snaps Vertical = **8**
- Graph Paper visibility is toggled **ON**
- Cells Horizontal = **8**
- Cells Vertical = **8**

4   Click the **Line** tool.

5   Work from top to bottom in the center two inches of the block. Begin at 3" on the top edge and draw 45 degree diagonal lines back and forth every two inches down the center (four lines).

Companion Book Three   **97**

Chapter 3: Divide and Conquer!

I find it much easier to create a *Prairie Braid* block by drawing the zigzag lines down the center first—it's a trait that they all have in common. It shows you right from the start how wide the strips will be, making the rest of the block easier to draw. And most importantly, it establishes the repeat of the patches.

6   On the left side of the zigzag lines, draw 45 degree lines up to the left from the third and fifth nodes to the block outline creating the diagonal strips on the left side of the block. Do the same on the right side of the block, but draw an additional diagonal in the bottom 1" of the lower-right corner.

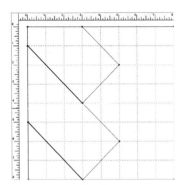

Step 6
Lines on left

7   Click **Add to Sketchbook** to save the block.

That's it for creating a square braid block that is repeatable! Try using this *Prairie Braid* block in borders or vertical strip quilts. Keep the blocks square to maintain the right angles of the strips. For quilts with odd dimensions use the Tiled Square border style to keep the blocks square.

Now let's take our repeatable *Prairie Braid* square block and transform it into a long strip block. You can use this block in a vertical strip layout with the strip of the same proportions. Print one long foundation pattern, gather your scraps and start sewing!

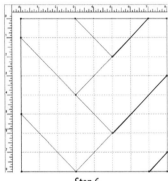

Step 6
Lines on right

8   Click **BLOCK > New Block > EasyDraw Block**.

9   On the Precision Bar, enter these values:

- Block Width = **8.00**
- Block Height = **48.00**
- Snaps Horizontal = **8**
- Snaps Vertical = **48**
- Graph Paper visibility is toggled **ON**
- Cells Horizontal = **8**
- Cells Vertical = **48**

Step 7
Add to Sketchbook

Step 8

Step 9

Drawing Prairie Braid Strips

98   EQ6 Pieced Drawing

Chapter 3: Divide and Conquer!

Step 10
Line

Step 11
Zoom In

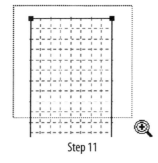

Step 11

10. Click the **Line** tool.

11. Click the **Zoom In** tool and drag a box to zoom in on the top-half of the block.

12. Count down eight divisions from the top of the block and draw a horizontal line across the block. Press the **SPACEBAR** to select the line you just drew, right-click, and choose **Convert to Guides**.

> **Note**
> You may want to change the color of the guidelines to contrast with the graph paper lines. Click on the **More Drawing Board Options** button for a shortcut to the Drawing Board Setup. Guideline color is listed under **Display**. I usually keep my graph paper lines teal and my guidelines red so I can see both easily.

13. Using the top 8 x 8 divisions, draw the repeatable *Prairie Braid* as in steps 1 through 6. Leave the bottom open, as illustrated.

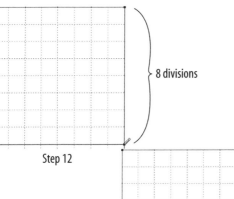

8 divisions

Step 12

Step 12

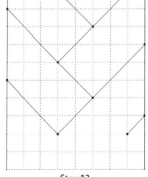

Step 13

Drawing Prairie Braid Strips

Companion Book Three   **99**

Chapter 3: Divide and Conquer!

14. Switch to the **Pick** tool and **Select All** (**CTRL+A**), then click on the **small red square** in the corner of the Pick took to bring up the Symmetry box.

Step 14
Pick

15. **Clone** the selection and move the clone down the block, eight divisions beneath the original, matching up the end nodes and making sure it snaps into place. While the clone is still selected, repeat **clone** *four* more times, moving each successive clone down the strip until you have filled the block. This strip has a total of six repeats. If you are still zoomed in you will need to scroll the window to move down the block.

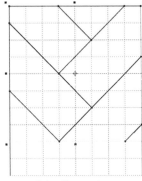
Symmetry Box

Select lines to clone

16. Click **Add to Sketchbook**.

Now that you have unlocked the mystery of how the *Prairie Braid* repeats you can create other variations. Here are a few for you to try. The first two variations use the same proportions as the braid in the exercise, except that I increased the snap points to 24 x 24 so that I could draw narrower strips. The third one has shorter wider strips and was drawn as a 6" x 8" block with snap points set at 24 x 32. Remember to draw the zigzag down the center first!

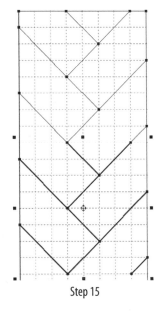
Step 15

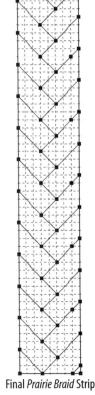

Variations of *Prairie Braid* Block

Step 16
Add to Sketchbook

Final *Prairie Braid* Strip

Chapter 3: Divide and Conquer!

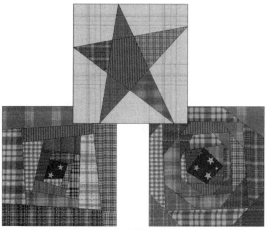

Examples of *Wacky Star*, *Wacky Cabin*, and *Wacky Pineapple* Blocks

Wacky Cabins, Stars & Pineapples

The Snap to Drawing option in EasyDraw™ is a feature that lets you draw lines more randomly to create crazy quilt type blocks and blocks with odd angles (I call these wacky blocks). Let's try out this feature while creating some fun and wacky-looking stars and log cabin blocks. These blocks are foundation piecing friendly!

1. Click **WORKTABLE > Work on Block**.

2. Click **BLOCK > New Block > EasyDraw Block**.

3. On the Precision Bar, enter these values pressing your keyboard TAB key after each:

   - Block Width = **6.00**
   - Block Height = **6.00**
   - Snaps Horizontal = **24**
   - Snaps Vertical = **24**
   - Graph Paper visibility is toggled **OFF**

Also on the Precision Bar, turn off **Snap to Grid**, leave Snap to Node on and turn on **Snap to Drawing**.

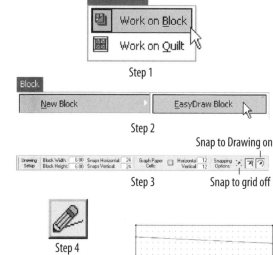

Step 1

Step 2

Step 3   Snap to grid off

Snap to Drawing on

Step 4
Line

Step 5

Step 6

IMPORTANT
When you are done with this exercise, remember to turn Snap to Grid back ON and turn Snap to Drawing OFF. Never leave Snap to Drawing on all the time. Only turn it on when you need to use it and then turn it off!

Make a Wacky Log Cabin

4. Click on the **Line** tool.

5. Begin by drawing a horizontal line across the block a little way from the top—from outline to outline. Don't worry about making it straight! This is Log #1.

6. Draw a vertical line beginning at the first log down to the bottom of the block. Make sure you begin on the first line, so that Snap to Drawing will create a node. This is Log #2.

Companion Book Three **101**

Chapter 3: Divide and Conquer!

7   Draw another horizontal line from Log #2 to the left side of the block. This is Log #3.

8   Draw another vertical line from Log #3 line to Log #1. This is Log #4.

9   Working clockwise, continue creating rounds of logs until you have a small wacky square in the center of the block. To keep an even number of logs on all sides, you will end with a vertical line on the left.

10 Add this *Wacky Log Cabin* to the Sketchbook by clicking the **Add to Sketchbook** button.

Make a Wacky Five-Point Star

11 Click **BLOCK > New Block > EasyDraw Block**. Keep the same drawing board setup as in step 3.

Have you ever drawn a five-point star with pencil and paper? This *Wacky Star* is created the same way.

12 Click on the **Line** tool.

13 Lines of this star will go from block outline to block outline. Draw the first line from top to bottom, beginning it slightly left of center and ending it an inch or so from the lower-left corner. Continue drawing the five-point star making sure to start the next line at the end node of the previous line (see illustration). Your star will not necessarily look like the example, but it will show you the direction to draw the lines. The last line ends on the same node you began.

14 Add this *Wacky Star* to the Sketchbook by clicking the **Add to Sketchbook** button.

Make a Wacky Pineapple

Wacky Pineapples are not hard to draw. They are made up of two basic shapes: wacky triangles and wacky strips!

15 Click **BLOCK > New Block > EasyDraw Block**. Keep the same drawing board setup as in step 3.

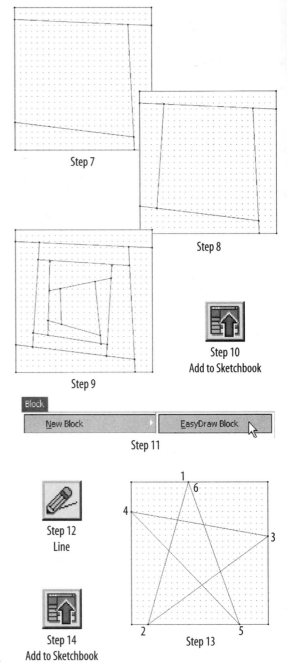

Chapter 3: Divide and Conquer!

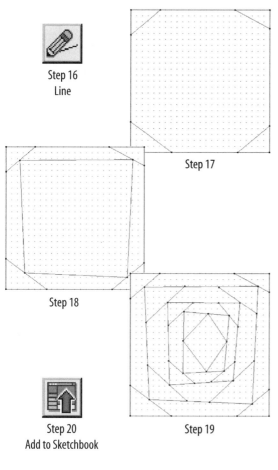

Step 16
Line

Step 17

Step 18

Step 20
Add to Sketchbook

Step 19

16 Click on the **Line** tool.

17 Draw diagonal lines in each of the four corners of the block. These lines create small lopsided triangles.

18 Working clockwise, and beginning and ending about midway on the long side of the triangles, draw a strip between the top two triangles. Begin the next strip on the end node of the previous line and continue drawing strips on the remaining three sides of the block. This will create a new wacky square in the center of the block.

19 Continue drawing four diagonal lines (creating triangles) followed by four strips until you have a small wacky square in the center. You can end with the strips or the triangles. Ending with triangles will make the center square on-point (in a wacky sort of way!).

20 Add this *Wacky Pineapple* to the Sketchbook by clicking the **Add to Sketchbook** button.

Make a Wacky Star Cabin or a Wacky Pineapple Star (or vice versa)!

To make a *Wacky Star Cabin* block, create a new *Wacky Cabin* block, but draw only two rounds of logs. Draw a *Wacky Five-Point Star* in the center.

To make a *Wacky Pineapple Star*, edit the *Wacky Star* you saved previously (or draw a new one). If the center of your saved star is small, you may want to draw one with a larger center. In the center of the star draw a five-sided pineapple. Drawing it works the same as a square pineapple (triangles in corners and strips on the sides) except you have five corners and sides.

Try creating some other wacky blocks. Here are a few examples; a *Wacky Sawtooth Star*, *Churn Dash* and *Shoo Fly* block. You might even want to add something wacky the center of the block!

Examples of *Wacky Sawtooth Star*, *Churn Dash*, and *Shoo Fly* Blocks

Companion Book Three **103**

Chapter 3: Divide and Conquer!

Drawing a Winding Ways Block

One of the fascinating characteristics of a *Winding Ways* block (also know as *Wheel of Mystery*) is the way it creates circles when set side-by-side in a quilt layout. In order for the design to create these perfect secondary circles, you need to start with perfect arcs. Let me show you how we can do it in EasyDraw™.

1   Click **WORKTABLE > Work on Block.**

2   Click **BLOCK > New Block > EasyDraw Block.**

3   On the Precision Bar, enter these values pressing your keyboard TAB key after each:

- Block Width = **12.00**
- Block Height = **12.00**
- Snaps Horizontal = **24**
- Snaps Vertical = **24**
- Graph Paper visibility is toggled **ON**
- Cells Horizontal = **2**
- Cells Vertical = **2**

*Be sure to turn **Snap to Grid** back **ON** and **Snap to Drawing OFF***

4   Click on the **Arc** tool.

5   Beginning in the upper-right corner of the block, draw an arc down the lower-left corner. Next, draw a mirror image arc beginning in the lower-left corner and ending in the upper-right. The arc pair should curve outward from the center. If the arcs are drawing in the other direction, press the **SPACEBAR** on your keyboard *while still drawing the arc* and it will flip the direction.

6   Draw a second pair of arcs in the opposite corners.

7   **Add to Sketchbook** to establish nodes where the arcs intersect.

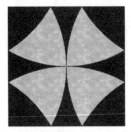

Example of *Winding Ways* Block

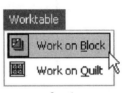

Step 1

Step 2

Step 3

Step 4
Arc

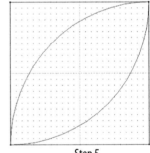

Step 5

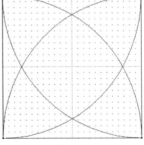

Step 6

Step 7
Add to Sketchbook

Chapter 3: Divide and Conquer!

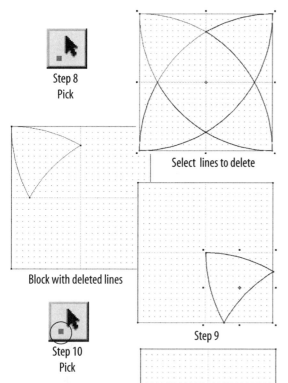

Step 8
Pick

Select lines to delete

Block with deleted lines

Step 9

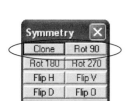

Step 10
Pick

Step 10
Click Clone then click Rot 90

Step 10
Move to lower-left quadrant

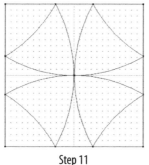

Step 11
Click Clone then click Rot 90

Step 11
Move to each adjacent quadrant

8 Using the **Pick** tool, select and delete all curves except those that are in the upper-left quadrant of the block. You can do this quickly by dragging a marquee around one section at a time and deleting them or by holding down the **DELETE** key and clicking on individual lines.

9 **Select All** (**CTRL+A**) to select the remaining curves and move them down to the lower-right quadrant of the block. Make sure the node on the upper-left point snaps exactly in the center of the block. Zoom in on the center if necessary. Keep the curves selected.

10 If it is not already showing, open the Symmetry menu box. You can click on the **small red square** on the **Pick** tool to open it quickly or right-click on the worktable and choose Symmetry. **Clone** the curves and **rotate 90 degrees** (**Rot 90**) and then move the clone over to the lower-left quadrant, again making sure the point node snaps in the center of the block.

11 *Repeat* this process (**clone** and **rotate 90 degrees**) *two more times*, moving each to the adjacent quadrant.

12 **Add to Sketchbook** to save the block.

Note
Color two *Winding Ways* blocks in opposing colors and alternate them in a horizontal quilt layout to get the full effect of the circles.

Drawing a Winding Ways Block

Companion Book Three **105**

Drawing Fan Blocks

Learn more about drawing and partitioning arcs in EasyDraw™ while making a fan block. We'll start with a simple fan block, but then we'll add and subtract parts to make several other variations.

1 Click **WORKTABLE > Work on Block.**

2 Click **BLOCK > New Block > EasyDraw Block**.

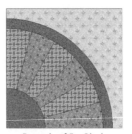

Example of *Fan* Block

3 On the Precision Bar, enter these values pressing your keyboard TAB key after each:

- Block Width = **12.00**
- Block Height = **12.00**
- Snaps Horizontal = **24**
- Snaps Vertical = **24**
- Graph Paper visibility is toggled **ON**
- Cells Horizontal = **12**
- Cells Vertical = **12**

Step 1

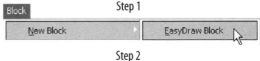

Step 2

Step 3

Step 4
Arc

4 Click on the **Arc** tool.

5 Draw a 4" arc in the lower-left corner starting at 8" on the left edge and ending at 4" on the bottom edge.

Note
If the arc is turned the wrong way, press the SPACEBAR while you are still drawing the arc and it will flip in the opposite direction.

6 Draw a 10" arc facing the same direction, starting at 2" on the left edge and ending at 10" on the bottom edge.

7 Click on the **Shape** tool, clicking on the **small red square** in the corner to bring up the Edit Arc box.

8 On the Edit Arc box, change the number beside Partition to **6**.

9 Click on the small arc and then click **Partition** on the Edit Arc box. *Repeat* this partitioning on the large arc.

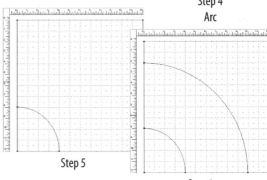

Step 5
Step 6

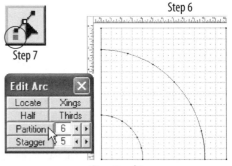

Step 7

Steps 8 and 9

Drawing Fan Blocks

106 *EQ6 Pieced Drawing*

Chapter 3: Divide and Conquer!

Step 10
Line

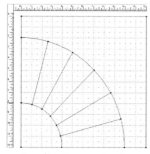

Draw lines to connect nodes

10 Switch to the **Line** tool and draw lines to connect the nodes between the arcs to create the fan blades.

11 **Add to Sketchbook**.

Let's add a ring to the outside of the fan. The traditional *Grandmother's Fan* usually has an added piping or trim at the outer edge of the fan, but we'll draw it as another arc.

12 Click on the **Arc** tool again and draw an arc 1" from the large arc.

13 **Add to Sketchbook**.

Now we'll partition the outer arc and try a couple more things for our fan.

Step 12
Arc

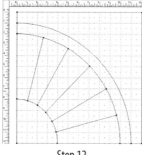

Step 12

14 Click the **small red square** on the **Shape** tool again bringing up the Edit Arc box. Partition the outer arc by **6**. Notice that EQ remembers the partition number from before. This holds true until you exit the project file.

15 Click on the **Line** tool.

16 Draw short lines from the nodes of the outer circle to the next larger circle extending the blades. Then draw a diagonal line in each of these outer sections.

Step 13
Add to Sketchbook

Step 14
Shape

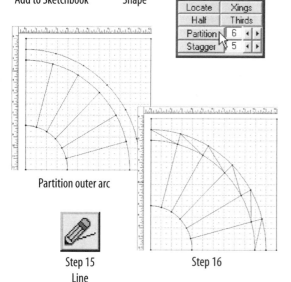

Partition outer arc

Step 15
Line

Step 16

Drawing Fan Blocks

Companion Book Three **107**

Chapter 3: Divide and Conquer!

17. Click on the **Pick** tool and hold down your keyboard **DELETE** key as you click the arc segments between the blades of the outer arcs to delete them. This creates a look of overlapping blades.

18. **Add to Sketchbook**.

> **Note**
> If you want to foundation piece the overlapping fan block, do not delete the outer arc segments. In the print foundation pattern dialog re-section the block so that the blade section is one group.

Let's try one more fan with petal tips.

19. Click the **View Sketchbook** button then select the fan saved in step 13, click **Edit** to place it on the worktable.

20. Click the **small red square** on the **Shape** tool, bringing up the Edit Arc box again. This time, change the number beside Stagger to **6**, click on the outer arc and then click on **Stagger**. Notice that using Stagger places the nodes halfway between the nodes on the adjacent arc.

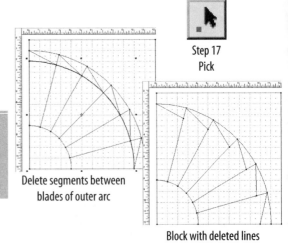

Step 17
Pick

Delete segments between blades of outer arc

Block with deleted lines

Step 18
Add to Sketchbook

Step 19
View Sketchbook

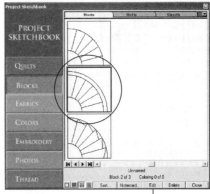

Click to select block Step 19

Step 20
Shape

Step 20

Chapter 3: Divide and Conquer!

Step 21
Arc

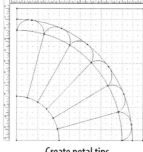
Create petal tips

Step 22
Pick

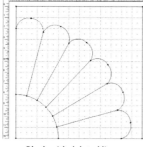
Block with deleted lines

Step 23
Add to Sketchbook

21   Click on the **Arc** tool and draw short arcs from the nodes of the second largest arc to the staggered nodes on the outer arc to create the petal tips.

22   Switch back to the **Pick** tool, hold down your keyboard **DELETE** key and click the arc segments between and inside the petals to delete them.

23   Click **Add to Sketchbook** to save this block.

Can you think of other ideas for your fans? Try partitioning by different numbers to make more or fewer blades or petals. You might also want to try a block with two fans like these pictured variations.

Variations of *Fan* Block

Chapter 3: Divide and Conquer!

Drawing a Dresden Plate Block

The *Dresden Plate* block can be made with any number of petals or blades, but the traditional *Dresden Plate* block has sixteen blades and a 3" center circle. This block is a good example of how deleting lines is part of the process of creating the finished block.

1   Click **WORKTABLE > Work on Block.**

2   Click **BLOCK > New Block > EasyDraw Block.**

3   On the Precision Bar, enter these values pressing your keyboard TAB key after each:

- Block Width = **15.00**
- Block Height = **15.00**
- Snaps Horizontal = **60**
- Snaps Vertical = **60**
- Graph Paper visibility is toggled **ON**
- Cells Horizontal = **15**
- Cells Vertical = **15**

When working on a block with an odd-numbered size I find it helpful to draw guidelines to help me find the center of the block. Let's do that first.

4   Click on the **Line** tool.

5   Draw a vertical and horizontal line in the center to divide the block into a four patch.

6   Click on the **Pick** tool.

7   **Select All** (**CTRL+A**), right-click and choose **Convert to Guides** from the context menu.

Example of *Dresden Plate* Block

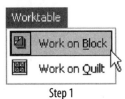

Step 1

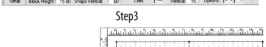

Step 2

Step 3

Step 4
Line

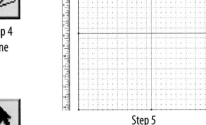

Step 5

Step 6
Pick

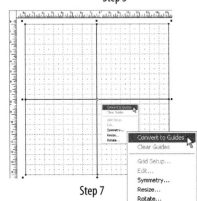

Step 7

Drawing a Dresden Plate Block

110   EQ6 Pieced Drawing

Chapter 3: Divide and Conquer!

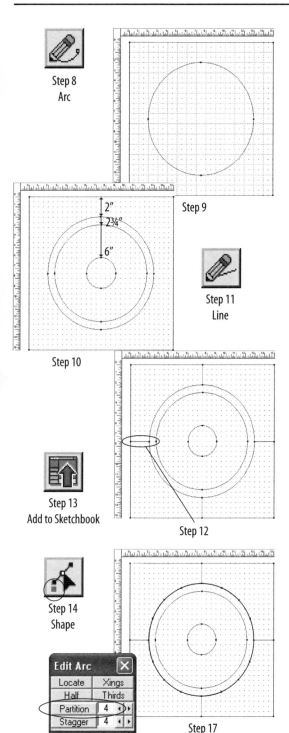

Step 8 — Arc
Step 9
Step 10
Step 11 — Line
Step 12
Step 13 — Add to Sketchbook
Step 14 — Shape
Step 17 — Partition outer arcs by 4

8   Click on the **Arc** tool.

9   Starting at the top center at 12:00 (12 o'clock) and working clockwise or counter-clockwise 2" in from the block outline, draw four arcs to make a circle. Arcs will begin and end at 12:00, 3:00, 6:00 and 9:00.

10 Measuring from the block outline, draw two more circles (four arcs each) at 2¾" and 6" inside the first circle. You should now have three circles. Once you have your circles drawn, you can *turn off the graph paper lines on the Precision Bar.*

Even though you cannot see them, there are four grid points per inch on the drawing board. This is equivalent to 1/4" for a 15" block.

11 Click on the **Line** tool.

12 Draw four short anchor lines from each of the connecting nodes on the largest circle to the block outline.

13 Click on the **Add to Sketchbook** button to save the block at this stage.

14 Click on the **Shape** tool, clicking on the **small red square** to bring up the Edit Arc box.

15 On the Edit Arc box, change the number beside Partition to **4** and then change the number beside Stagger to **4**.

16 Click on one of the arcs of the largest circle to select it.

17 On the Edit Arc box, click on **Partition** to partition this arc into four segments. *Repeat* this partitioning with the remaining three arcs of the outer circle.

Drawing a Dresden Plate Block

Companion Book Three   **111**

Chapter 3: Divide and Conquer!

18. Click on one of the arcs of second largest circle.

19. On the Edit Arc box, click on **Stagger** to segment the arc. *Repeat* with the remaining three arcs of this circle. Notice that using Stagger places the nodes halfway between the nodes we added to the largest circle.

20. Click on one of the arcs of smallest circle.

21. On the Edit Arc box, click on **Stagger**. *Repeat* with the remaining three arcs of this circle.

22. Click on the **Line** tool.

23. On the Precision Bar, turn off **Snap to Grid**. (Turning Snap to Grid off will make it easier for lines to snap to the nodes and not the grid points.)

24. Draw lines to connect the nodes between the smallest circle and the second largest circle to form the 16 blades of the *Dresden Plate*, skipping the nodes where the arcs connect.

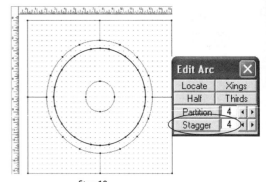

Step 19
Stagger middle arcs by 4

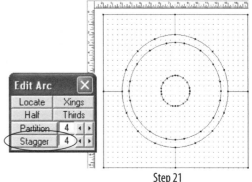

Step 21
Stagger inner arcs by 4

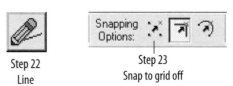

Step 22
Line

Step 23
Snap to grid off

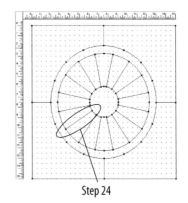

Step 24

Chapter 3: Divide and Conquer!

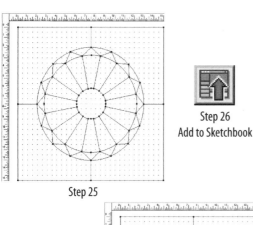

Step 25

Step 26
Add to Sketchbook

Step 27
Pick

Step 28
Select lines to delete

Step 29
Add to Sketchbook

Block with deleted lines

25 To create the points on top of the blades, start at 12:00 and draw lines in a zigzag manner going back and forth between the nodes of the two outer circles.

26 Click **Add to Sketchbook** to save the block at this stage.

At this stage of our block construction, you can see the *Dresden Plate* design. Now we need to delete the parts of the drawing that are not needed in the final block.

27 Click on the **Pick** tool.

28 Delete all the arc segments of the two outer circles. You can do this one at a time by selecting each one and pressing **DELETE** on the keyboard or you can hold down the **DELETE** key and click on the curves one right after the other to delete them. When you are finished deleting the curves, the block is complete.

29 **Add to Sketchbook** to save your block.

IMPORTANT
Turn Snap to Grid back on when you are done with this exercise!

Try creating other variations of the *Dresden Plate* block. You might want to try one with more or fewer blades or you might want to create one with a larger center circle for a sunflower look.

To make a *Dresden Plate* with curved petals, use the Arc tool and draw two arcs on top of each section to form the petals. See the previous fan exercise if you need more details on how to do this. By the way, you can also alternate between petals and blades!

Note
If you reverse the Partition and Stagger on the circles, the center lines of the block will be between the blades rather than in the center of the blade. See some of the *Dresden Plate* blocks in the EQ6 Block Library under 1 Classic Pieced for examples.

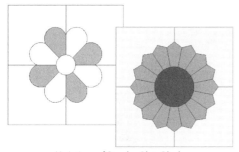

Variations of *Dresden Plate* Block

Companion Book Three

Chapter 3: Divide and Conquer!

Drawing a Mariner's Compass Block

This exercise shows you how to draw a traditional style of the *Mariner's Compass* block. There are many, many variations of this block, but most have one thing in common; four points of the compass should point North, South, East and West.

1   Click **WORKTABLE > Work on Block**.

2   Click **BLOCK > New Block > EasyDraw Block**.

3   On the Precision Bar, enter these values pressing your keyboard TAB key after each:

- Block Width = **12.00**
- Block Height = **12.00**
- Snaps Horizontal = **48**
- Snaps Vertical = **48**
- Graph Paper visibility is toggled **ON**
- Cells Horizontal = **12**
- Cells Vertical = **12**

4   Click on the **Arc** tool.

5   Starting 1/2" in from the block outline at 12:00 (12 o'clock), draw four arcs to make a circle.

6   *Measuring from the block outline* and going from the larger to the smaller, draw three more circles (four arcs each) at 2", 3" and 4½" inside the first one. Once you have your circles drawn, you can ***turn off the graph paper lines.***

7   Click on the **Line** tool.

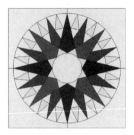

Example of *Mariner's Compass* Block

Step 1

Step 2

Step 3

Step 4
Arc

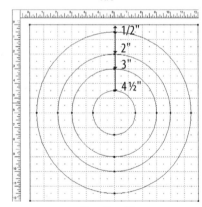

Steps 5 and 6

Step 7
Line

114   EQ6 Pieced Drawing

Chapter 3: Divide and Conquer!

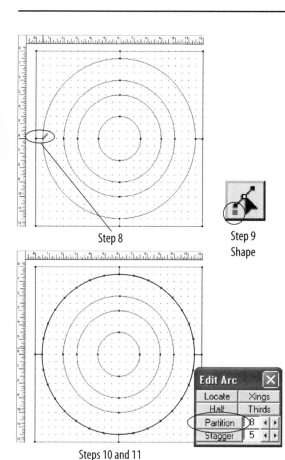

Step 8

Step 9
Shape

Steps 10 and 11

8   Draw four short anchor lines from the center nodes where the arcs connect, to the block outline.

9   Click on the **Shape** tool, clicking on the **small red square** on the button to bring up the Edit Arc box.

10 On the Edit Arc box, change the number beside Partition to **8**.

11 Click on each of the arcs of the largest circle and then click on **Partition** on the Edit Arc box.

12 Next, click on each arc of the small center circle and then click on **Half** on the Edit Arc box.

13 Click on the **Snap to Grid** button to turn it off.

14 Click on the **Line** tool.

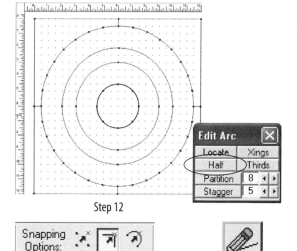

Step 12

Step 13
Snap to grid off

Step 14
Line

Drawing a Mariner's Compass

Companion Book Three   **115**

Chapter 3: Divide and Conquer!

15. Skipping *every other* node on the inner circle, draw the four long compass points extending to the outer circle, then back to the inner circle to create the North, South, East and West points, as shown.

16. Using the remaining nodes on the inner circle, draw four more long compass points to the outer circle, centering them between the first four.

17. Click on **Add to Sketchbook** to establish nodes for the next round of compass points.

18. Drawing from the newly established nodes to the outer circle, draw compass points between each of the existing points (eight total).

19. Click on **Add to Sketchbook** again.

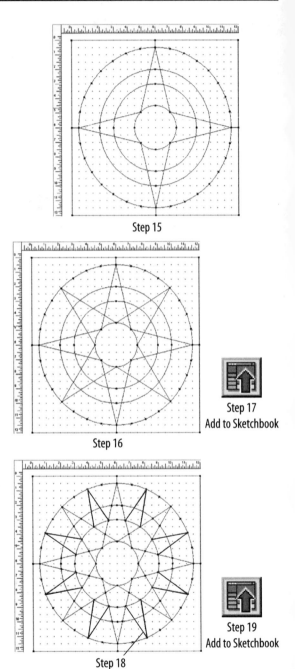

Step 15

Step 16

Step 17
Add to Sketchbook

Step 18

Step 19
Add to Sketchbook

116   EQ6 Pieced Drawing

Chapter 3: Divide and Conquer!

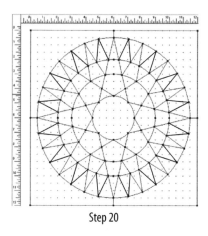

Step 20

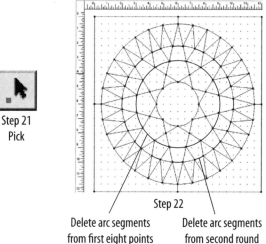

Step 22

Delete arc segments from first eight points

Delete arc segments from second round of points

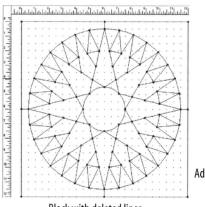

Block with deleted lines

Step 21 Pick

Step 23 Add to Sketchbook

20 Again drawing from the newly established nodes, draw compass points between each of the existing ones (sixteen total).

The compass design is complete now, but the block is not finished until we delete many of the lines we used to create it.

21 Click on the **Pick** tool.

22 Delete the arc segments in the first eight compass points. Then go back and delete the arc lines that are in the second round of compass points. To do this, hold down your keyboard **DELETE** key and click each arc and line you want to delete. You may need to click on the **Refresh** tool after each delete to clean up the screen trash left behind as you delete. Click **EDIT > Undo** if you accidentally delete the wrong line.

23 Click **Add to Sketchbook** to save this block.

Note
Be sure to turn Snap to Grid back on when you are finished with this exercise.

Here are a few variations using the same block setup. The oval compass is made by just changing the block size. Try one!

Variations of *Mariner's Compass* Block

Companion Book Three **117**

From Compass to Foundation

Do you prefer to foundation piece your compass blocks? Let me show you how to change the compass block created in the previous exercise to a foundation piece-able block!

Step 3 Pick — Step 4 Line

1. First, if you have not done so already, create the *Mariner's Compass* block from the previous exercise on page 114.

2. Retrieve the *Mariner's Compass* block from the Sketchbook and place it on the worktable.

3. Click on the **Pick** tool and hold down your keyboard **DELETE** key as you click the curve segments within the smallest outer points to delete them. Alternatively, you could select these and convert them to guides.

4. Using the **Line** tool, draw straight lines to replace the curves you just deleted. You may find it less confusing to work on just one quarter of the block at a time. **Zoom in** on the area if necessary.

5. **Add to Sketchbook** when you are done.

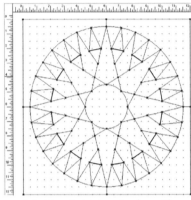

Select lines to delete and replace with straight lines

Step 5 Add to Sketchbook

That's really all we need to do to make this particular compass foundation piecing friendly! However, since we still have curved seams in part of the block, we will have to help EQ6 print the foundation the way we want it. If you are familiar with Judy Mathieson's* method of making compass blocks, the compass is foundation pieced and then is either appliquéd on or stitched to the background similar to a *Drunkard's Path* block. The center circles are usually also appliquéd. In other words, the outer and inner curves are left intact. Let me show you how we can section our edited block to make a usable foundation pattern.

Step 6

> **Note**
> Be sure to name your block on the Notecard so that you can easily identify it as the one to use for a foundation pattern!

6. Click **FILE > Print > Foundation pattern**.

7. When the Print dialog comes up it will show the **Numbering** tab and you will see your block with no numbers.

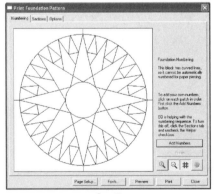

Step 7 Numbering Tab

Chapter 3: Divide and Conquer!

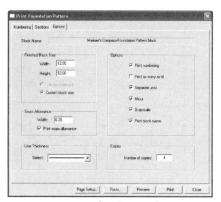

Step 8
Options Tab

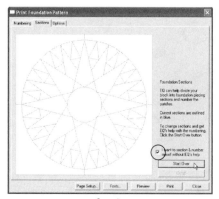

Step 9
Sections Tab

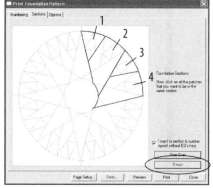

Step 10
Group patches as shown

8   Click on the **Options** tab first and change the block size to **12.00 x 12.00**. Change the other settings to match the options you see here.

9   Click on the **Sections** tab. Down on the right, check the box beside *I want to section & number myself without EQ's help*. Then click **Start Over**.

Since this is a symmetrical block, we can make our regrouping easier by only doing one quarter of the block. Once we have this quarter sectioned we can print four copies of the page to get all the foundations we need to make the block.

10   On the **Sections** tab image of the compass block, start regrouping the sections in the quarter to the right of the 12:00 compass point. Click the patches as shown; clicking on the **Group** button after each section is highlighted. There are *four* sections: two smaller ones and two larger ones. Be sure to include the small triangle along the inside circle when you group the larger sections. Don't worry about the background or the center circle. We'll deal with those later.

Notes
- **If you make a mistake when clicking on patches before you click on Group, you can undo by holding down the SHIFT key and clicking on the patch to deselect it.**
- **If you make a mistake but have already clicked on Group, just click the Start Over button and repeat Step 10 following the image to the left.**

Companion Book Three   **119**

Chapter 3: Divide and Conquer!

11. When you are done grouping these sections, click on the **Numbering** tab. The numbering is a little more involved. The sections/units will be outlined in green. We have to click on the patches to renumber them ourselves. Click the **Add Numbers** button. Working on one section at a time, click the patches in the order shown to number them for easier foundation piecing. EQ will automatically add the unit letters for you.

12. Click on **Preview** to view your new sections. Since we set the size at 12", all four sections should be on one page. But you may need to move them apart a little. We have created two repeats of the compass point foundations and there are eight of these repeats per block. You only need to print this page four times. Click **Close** twice to return to the Block worktable.

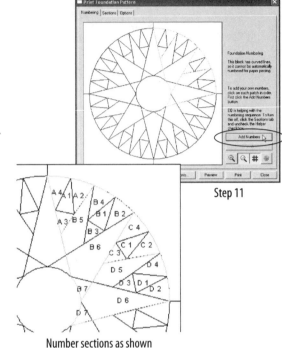

Step 11

Number sections as shown

Step 12

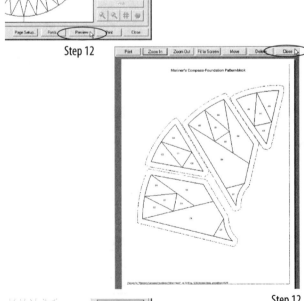

Step 12

Step 12

Chapter 3: Divide and Conquer!

Step 13
Save

Step 14

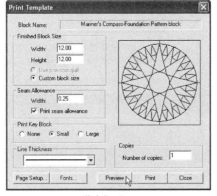

Click Preview

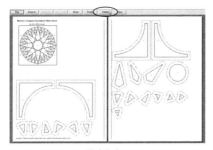

Click Delete

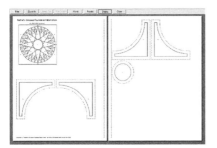

Pages with only the desired templates

13 Now, before you do anything further, click on the **Save** button on the main toolbar. If you've named your project file, you won't see anything happen, but this little trick will save your foundation's new grouping and numbering. When you use the foundation pattern again, you won't have to start all over!

14 To get the patterns for the background and center circle, use **FILE > Print > Templates**. Click the **Preview** button, click the **Delete** button on top of the screen, then click on each to delete everything except the templates for these patches. If you plan to appliqué the compass, just cut a 12½" square for the background.

Foundation Piecing Tip
When you piece the foundations, you will piece each lettered unit first and then sew the smaller units to the adjacent larger ones (e.g. stitch unit A to unit B). When those are together, stitch together the eight repeats into pairs and then stitch the pairs together.

*Judy Mathieson has authored two books dedicated to Mariner's Compass blocks: *Mariner's Compass Quilts: New Directions* (1995) and *Mariner's Compass Quilts: Setting a New Course* (2005), both published by C&T Publishing, Inc. I highly recommend especially the newest book if you plan to make a lot of compasses.

Chapter 3: Divide and Conquer!

Drawing a Circle of Geese Block

One of the basic shapes of quilting—the triangle—takes off in a new direction in this block!

1. Click **WORKTABLE > Work on Block.**

2. Click **BLOCK > New Block > EasyDraw Block**.

3. On the Precision Bar, enter these values pressing your keyboard TAB key after each:

   - Block Width = **6.00**
   - Block Height = **6.00**
   - Snaps Horizontal = **48**
   - Snaps Vertical = **48**
   - Graph Paper visibility is toggled **ON**
   - Cells Horizontal = **6**
   - Cells Vertical = **6**

4. Click on the **Line** tool.

5. Draw a horizontal line and vertical line dividing the block into a four patch block.

6. Click on the **Arc** tool.

We'll draw just one quarter of the geese circle and then we can use Clone and Rotate to make the completed block.

7. Draw two arcs in the upper-left quarter of the block. Drawing from right to left, draw the first arc beginning it at the horizontal center of the block 1/4" from the top and ending it at the vertical center 1/4" from the left side of the block. Draw the second arc, beginning it at 1½" from the top center and ending at 1½" from the left center.

8. Click the **Add to Sketchbook** button to establish nodes where the arcs meet the center lines.

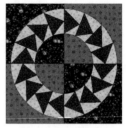

Example of *Circle of Geese* Block

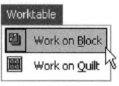

Step 1

Step 2

Step 3

Step 4
Line

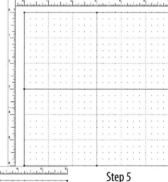

Step 5

Step 6
Arc

Step 8
Add to Sketchbook

Step 7

Chapter 3: Divide and Conquer!

Step 9
Shape

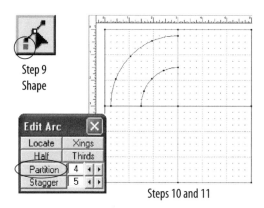

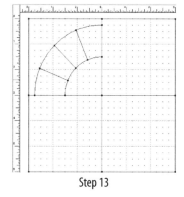
Steps 10 and 11

Step 12
Line

Step 14
Add to Sketchbook

Step 13

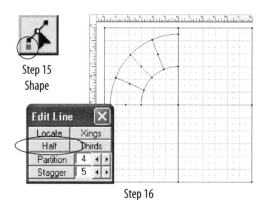
Step 16

Step 17
Line

Step 18
Snap to grid off

9 Click on the **Shape** tool, clicking on the **small red square** to bring up the Edit Arc box.

10 On the Edit Arc box, change the number beside Partition to **4**.

11 Click on the first arc to select it and then click on **Partition**. *Repeat* with the second arc so that both arcs are partitioned into 4 segments.

12 Click on the **Line** tool.

13 Drawing across from arc to arc, draw lines to connect nodes and create four fan blades.

14 Click **Add to Sketchbook**. This will establish nodes where the arcs meet the center lines. You will also have the block saved at this stage in case you want to try something different later.

Next, we need to add a node on the lines between the arcs so that we will have a center point to draw the small geese triangles.

15 Click on the **Shape** tool, clicking on the **small red square** to bring up the Edit Line box.

16 Click on one of the straight lines between the arcs. Then, on the Edit box, click on **Half**. (Notice that the title of the Edit box changes to Edit Line when a line is selected with the Shape tool). This will add a node in the center of the line. *Repeat* with the remaining four straight lines, including the two segments that fall along the horizontal and vertical center lines. There are 5 lines total to which we want to add a node. You cannot multiple-select lines to segment, so you must select each one separately and then click on **Half**.

17 Click on the **Line** tool.

18 Turn *off* Snap to Grid.

Drawing a Circle of Geese Block

Companion Book Three **123**

Chapter 3: Divide and Conquer!

19 Draw the two angled lines in each section to make four geese triangles between the arcs. You can have your geese flying clockwise or counter-clockwise, that's up to you! Once you have them drawn, click **Add to Sketchbook**.

20 **Turn Snap to Grid back on.**

21 Click on the **Pick** tool, clicking on the **small red square** to bring up the Symmetry box.

22 Point to the drawing and drag a selection box around the entire upper-left quadrant so that the arcs and geese are selected. This selects a little more than we need, so we need to deselect some of the lines. Hold down the **SHIFT** key and click all the segments that are part of the vertical and horizontal four patch to deselect them. The arc should be open ended as shown (or you could begin by holding down the **SHIFT** key and click on all the lines of the arc-geese, but that takes a little longer to do than the selection box and deleting method described above.)

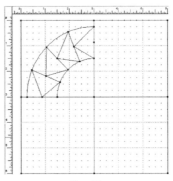
Step 19

Add to Sketchbook

Step 20
Snap to grid on

Step 21
Pick

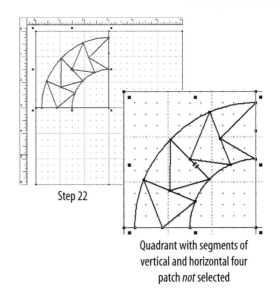
Step 22

Quadrant with segments of vertical and horizontal four patch *not* selected

Chapter 3: Divide and Conquer!

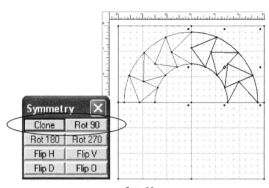

Step 23

23   On the Symmetry box, click on **Clone** and then immediately click on **Rot 90**. Move the cloned section to the upper-right quadrant, aligning the nodes carefully and making sure the clone snaps into place when you release the mouse. Keep the newest section selected and then *repeat* the **Clone** and **Rot 90** process *two more times*, moving each new section to its respective quadrant to complete the block.

24   Once all parts are snapped into place, you can add the final block in the Sketchbook by clicking **Add to Sketchbook**.

Now that you know the process, try some of your own variations of this circular geese block. Try varying the width of the arcs and adding more geese if you like. You could even draw more than one circle of geese on one block or vary the direction they are flying.

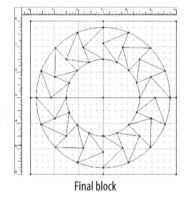

Final block

Step 24
Add to Sketchbook

> **Note**
> Foundation piecing is the preferred method for sewing these geese arcs. The rest of the block construction would be similar to piecing a *Drunkard's Path* block. On the Section tab of the Print Foundation dialog, regroup the sections so that each quarter ring of geese is one group and each separate background area is a one-piece group.

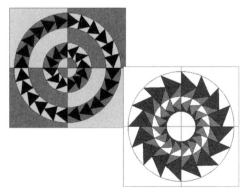

Variations of *Circle of Geese* Block

Chapter 3: Divide and Conquer!

Drawing Curved Geese

This exercise will show you how to make a longer curve of geese that is suitable for borders. It has a nice smooth curve that will repeat if you set it in a border or if you want your geese to fly across the quilt.

1. Click on **WORKTABLE > Work on Block**.

2. Click **BLOCK > New Block > EasyDraw Block**.

3. On the Precision Bar, enter these values pressing your keyboard TAB key after each:
   - Block Width = **6.00**
   - Block Height = **12.00**
   - Snaps Horizontal = **24**
   - Snaps Vertical = **48**
   - Graph Paper visibility is toggled **ON**
   - Cells Horizontal = **6**
   - Cells Vertical = **12**

4. Click on the **Arc** tool.

In the next three steps, as needed, press the **SPACEBAR** before releasing the mouse to make the arc flip in the opposite direction.

5. Draw a right facing arc beginning at the top of the block 1" from the left to the graph paper intersection at 2" horizontal and 3" vertical.

6. Draw a second arc, this time left facing, beginning at the end node of the first arc and ending at 2" horizontal and 9" vertical.

7. Draw a third arc, again right facing, from the end node of the second arc to the bottom of the block 1" from the left.

Notice that we've made the central arc twice as long as the top and bottom arcs. If you are trying to create a repeating curve, this is important to remember.

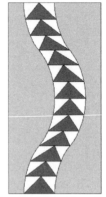

Example of *Curved Geese* Block

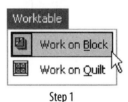

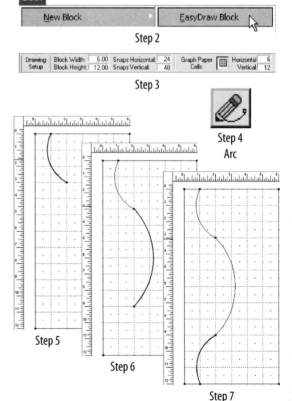

Chapter 3: Divide and Conquer!

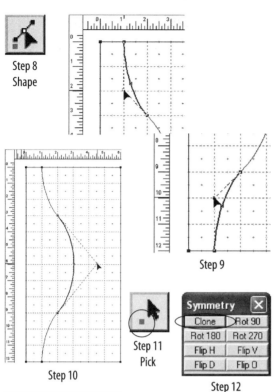

Step 8 Shape

Step 9

Step 10

Step 11 Pick

Step 12

Step 13 Add to Sketchbook

Step 14 Shape

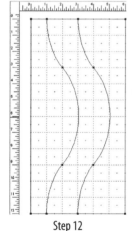

Step 12

Step 15

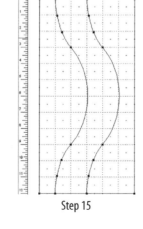

Step 15

Although this initial curve is symmetrical, it's not smooth. If you set this block end to end you would end up with a v-shape where the lines meet together. To fix this we need to smooth our curve so that it is contained within a 2" column. The graph paper lines make this easy.

8   Click on the **Shape** tool.

9   Hold down the **SHIFT** key and select the top and bottom arcs so that you can see the handle tent on both at the same time. Grab the handle of the top arc and move it so that it rests 2" down from the top and is parallel to the top node. *Repeat* this with the bottom arc making it a mirror image of the top arc.

10 Select the center arc. Move the handle tent to the left so that the center node of the arc rests at the center of the block (3" from the left).

The entire curve should be contained within a 2" column now. It's a symmetrical curve that will repeat nicely if we set the blocks in a border.

Note
Although we can build smooth curves with arcs in EasyDraw™ please, remember that they are separate arcs. They can easily be separated at the nodes so you need to be careful to keep them connected.

Be sure to save this block when indicated in the next steps so that you can try the variations at the end of the exercise.

11 Click on the **Pick** tool, bringing up the Symmetry box. **Select All (CTRL+A)** to select all arcs.

12 **Clone** the curve and **move** the new curve over 2" to the right so that the top and bottom nodes snap into place at the center.

13 **Add to Sketchbook**.

14 Click on the **small red square** on the **Shape** tool, bringing up the Edit Arc box.

15 Click on each of the two top arcs separately and then click on **Thirds** on the Edit Arc box. *Repeat* with the bottom two arcs.

Companion Book Three   **127**

Chapter 3: Divide and Conquer!

16. On the Edit Arc box, change the number beside Partition to **6**.

17. Click each of the center arcs separately and then click on **Partition**.

18. Click on the **Line** tool. Draw a horizontal line from node to node between the two curves. At this stage it looks like a curvy ladder.

19. **Add to Sketchbook**.

20. Click on the **small red square** on the **Shape** tool again, bringing up the Edit Arc box. Click on each horizontal line between the curves and partition by clicking **Half**.

21. Click on the **Line** tool and draw two diagonal lines to the center node on each horizontal line to create the triangle geese shape. All the geese in this block are flying to the North (points up).

Note
The diagonal lines for the top and bottom geese rely on Snap to Grid. You can draw these first and then turn off Snap to Grid to draw the lines for the remaining geese.

22. When you have all the geese completed, click **Add to Sketchbook** again to save your new block.

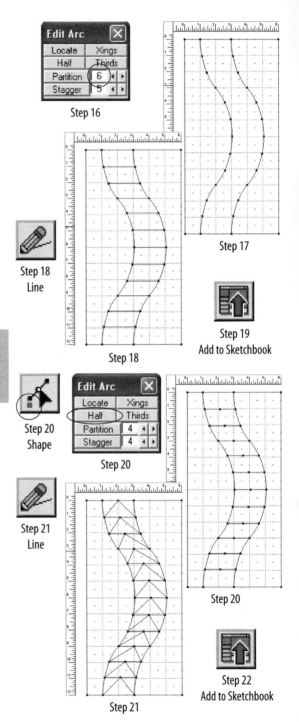

Chapter 3: Divide and Conquer!

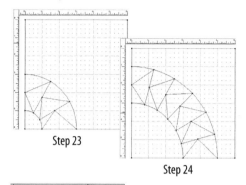

Step 23

Step 24

Make a Matching Corner Block for Geese Curves

To create a matching corner block for borders, place a new EasyDraw™ block on the worktable with block size at **6.00 x 6.00**, snap points at **24 x 24** and graph paper at **6 x 6**. You will want to create two of these corner blocks. The one you use will depend on how you have rotated the geese curve in the border.

23 For the first corner block draw a 1" and a 3" arc in the bottom-left corner of the block. Partition each arc by clicking **Thirds**. Draw the geese in the same manner as in steps 18-21.

24 For the second corner block draw a 3" and a 5" arc in the lower-left corner. **Partition by 6** and then draw the geese as before.

Use the small corner when center curve faces out, use the large corner block when the curve faces in.

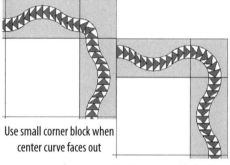

Use small corner block when center curve faces out

Use large corner block when the center curve faces in

You can use this same idea to create a *Curved Sawtooth* block. Try building other smooth curves in EasyDraw™ and see what you can come up with. Try varying the width at the top and bottom to get a three dimensional effect. The number of geese is up to you!

> **Note**
> Make a foundation pattern! When you go to print the Foundation Pattern, on the Sections tab, group all the pieces of the long geese curve together and then group each background patch separately. Renumbering the foundation is optional, since a long string of geese must always be paper pieced from the base to point.

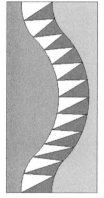

Variations of *Curved Geese* Blocks

Drawing Curved Geese

Companion Book Three

Chapter 3: Divide and Conquer!

Drawing a Giant Dahlia Block

The *Giant Dahlia* block is actually meant to be made as a whole quilt. Drawing it in EQ6 will give you precision templates for making it. Even if you never *sew* one of these beauties, the skills you learn as you draw it will be very helpful for other challenging blocks.

1. Click on **WORKTABLE > Work on Block**.

2. Click **BLOCK > New Block > EasyDraw Block**.

3. On the Precision Bar, enter these values pressing your keyboard TAB key after each:

    - Block Width = **12.00**
    - Block Height = **12.00**
    - Snaps Horizontal = **48**
    - Snaps Vertical = **48**
    - Graph Paper visibility is toggled **ON**
    - Cells Horizontal = **12**
    - Cells Vertical = **12**

Note
We'll be drawing the *Giant Dahlia* as a 12" block, but remember you can print it any size you need for templates.

4. Click on the **Arc** tool.

5. Measuring in from the block outline, draw three circles (four arcs each) at **1/2"**, **4½"** and **4¾"**. Once you have the circles drawn, you can *turn off the graph paper lines*.

6. Click on the **Shape** tool, clicking on the **small red square** to bring up the Edit Arc box.

7. On the Edit Arc box, change the number beside Partition and Stagger to **4**.

8. Select each arc of the outermost and the second largest circle separately, and then on the Edit Arc box click on **Partition** for each arc.

Example of *Giant Dahlia* Block

Step 1

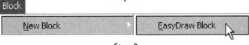
Step 2

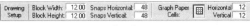
Step 3

Step 4
Arc

Step 5

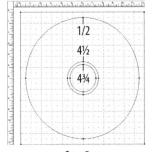
Step 5

Step 6
Shape

Step 8

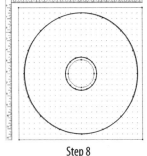
Step 8
Select arcs to Partition

130 EQ6 Pieced Drawing

Chapter 3: Divide and Conquer!

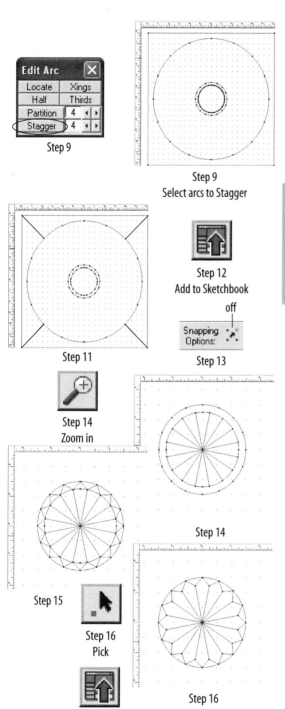

9. Select the arcs of the innermost circle and then click on **Stagger**.

10. Click on the **Line** tool.

11. Draw diagonal lines from each corner of the block to the corresponding node at 45 degrees on the outer circle. These are our anchor lines to connect the dahlia to the block outline.

12. **Add to Sketchbook**.

> **Note**
> Whenever you have a circle that is floating inside a block, you need to add at least two anchor lines to connect it to the block outline. These can be drawn on the diagonal like we did for this block, or at the center top, bottom or on the sides. EQ needs these anchor lines to define the background patches correctly.

13. *Turn off Snap to Grid*.

Notice that the center of the *Giant Dahlia* is a small *Dresden Plate*. We'll draw that first.

14. **Zoom in** on the center to make it easier to see. Draw **sixteen lines** from the nodes on the innermost circle to the center of the block, ignoring the nodes where the arcs connect.

15. Draw the triangle points on top of each blade going in a zigzag manner between the nodes of two circles.

16. Click on the **Pick** tool. **Select** and **delete** all of the arcs of the *innermost* circle only. Leave the remaining arcs around the *Dresden Plate* center until we create the petals of our dahlia. Removing them too soon makes the block unstable.

17. **Add to Sketchbook**.

Chapter 3: Divide and Conquer!

The spiral design of the *Giant Dahlia* is created by drawing overlapping petal shapes. It's not difficult, but it can be confusing if you get them out of order. Be sure to work in a clockwise direction as you draw the petals to keep from getting lost!

18 Click on the **Arc** tool.

19 Beginning on the point at #1 (see illustration) on the *Dresden Plate* center, draw an arc to the node at 12:00 (12 o'clock) on the outer circle (press the **SPACEBAR** on your keyboard if the arc is flipped the wrong direction). Draw a second arc from 12:00 to the point at #3 on the center. Note that the arcs begin and end **every sixth node** on the *Dresden Plate* center.

20 Draw a second petal, beginning at the next clockwise point of the center and ending six points away. Continue drawing this way in a clockwise manner until you have all 16 petals.

You will begin to see the spiral pattern of the patches once you get around to about 9:00. Look back on your drawing after every few petals and if the spiral seems askew, you may need to delete and redraw some of the petals.

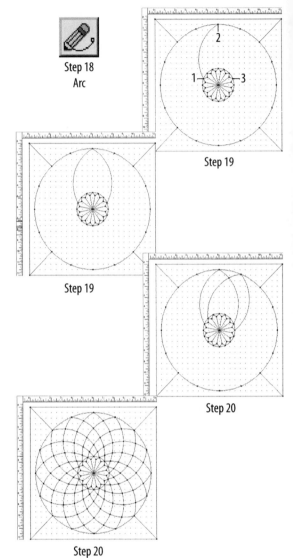

Step 18
Arc

Step 19

Step 19

Step 20

Step 20

132   EQ6 Pieced Drawing

Chapter 3: Divide and Conquer!

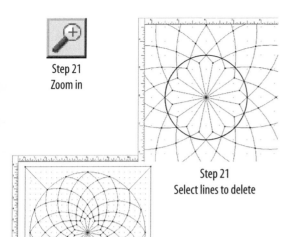

Step 21
Zoom in

Step 21
Select lines to delete

Final block

Step 22
Add to Sketchbook

21 When you have finished all sixteen petals, **zoom in** and **delete** the arcs between the *Dresden* points.

22 **Add** your finished *Giant Dahlia* to the **Sketchbook**.

One of the things I like best about this block is the fun we have in coloring it. Try using a shaded palette of solid colors in graduated values or create your own shaded palette of batiks and marbled fabrics from the Fabric Library.

Some *Giant Dahlias* have another set of petals between the outermost ring of petals of the design. To draw these additional petals you will need to partition each arc segment in half between the petals along the outer circle. Draw the arcs as illustrated to create the new petals. **Add to Sketchbook** and then go back and delete the segments of the arcs not needed.

Try a different center for the dahlia by having just a plain circle in the center. Try fewer petals or more petals. In other words…have fun with it!

See the Pieced PatchDraw Show & Draw Arc Grid section on page 37 for a totally different way to create a dahlia-type block with straight lines! It's the 5th variation.

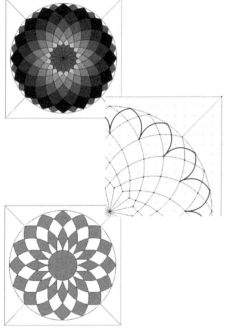

Variations of *Giant Dahlia* Block

Drawing a Giant Dahlia Block

Companion Book Three **133**

Drawing Outside the Box

I get many requests on how to draw 45° star blocks and 60° hexagonal blocks. There are a lot of variations in the Block Library, but everyone wants to know how to create their own. The majority of this chapter will concentrate on 45° and 60° blocks, but that's not all we will cover in this last chapter! I'll show you how to draw a complex foundation pattern. We'll learn to manipulate nodes to create a ball with swirl effects and a frame block with perspective. We'll also play with inset and offset blocks. Curious? Read on…

Drawing a Complex Foundation Block 136
Creating an Inset Block 145
Creating an Offset Shadow Block 148
Exercising with Node Select All 151
Drawing a Perspective Window
Frame Block 153
Eight Slices of a Circle 157
Drawing a Rolling Stone Block 161
Drawing Eight-Bladed Pinwheels 165
Drawing a Rising Sun Block 171
Going Crazy for Eights 175
Conquering the Radiant Star 176
Drawing 60° Blocks 182
Drawing Hexagonal Stars 188
Drawing a Seven Sisters Block 192
Drawing 3-D Cubes 194
Tessellating 60's 196
Drawing Hexagonal Blocks with
Pieced PatchDraw 199

Chapter 4

Chapter 4: Drawing Outside the Box

Drawing a Complex Foundation Block —Sweet Gum Leaf

What better subject to practice our foundation pattern drawing with than a nice leaf? Complex foundations are much easier if you have a picture to trace, so I will show you a quick way to get a picture to trace right from EQ6. This exercise will take your foundation pattern designing to a new level!

1   First let's get the leaf image to trace. We're going to use an appliqué block from EQ6's Block Library. Click **LIBRARIES > Block Library**. Then click **EQ6 Libraries > 6 Motifs > Leaves**. Add the *Sweet Gum* leaf to the Sketchbook. Click **Close**.

2   Click the **View Sketchbook** button, then click **Blocks**. Click the **Motifs** tab and choose the *Sweet Gum* leaf. Click **Edit** to place it on the worktable.

Example of *Sweet Gum Leaf* Block

Step 1

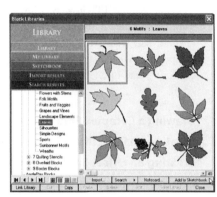

Step 2
Add *Sweet Gum* leaf to Sketchbook

Step 2
Select motif to edit

Chapter 4: Drawing Outside the Box

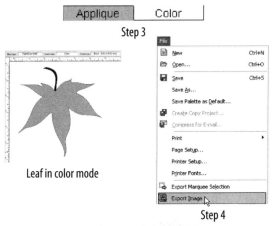

Step 3

Leaf in color mode

Step 4

Navigate to *My EQ6* folder

Create a new folder called *Images*

Double-click *Images* folder to open

Save newly named file

Step 5

3   Click on the **Color** tab. The leaf is lighter in color so it will be easy to trace. You can color another color if you like, but keep it light. You are coloring it for tracing purposes only.

4   Click **FILE > Export Image**. In the Export dialog, click the down arrow next to *Save in*. If it's not already there, navigate to the **My Documents\My EQ6** folder. Create a new folder here and call it **Images**. This is where we want to save our image. Double-click to open the **Images** folder. Type in *sweetgumleaf* in *File name* box. Click the down arrow beside *Save As Type* and choose **PNG**. Click on the **Save** button when you are done. (You can save the image in another format if you like, but I like the quality better of a PNG.)

Note
You can add the Export Image button, as well as others, to the Project toolbar. See the toolbar reference on page 213.

5   In the next dialog you get to choose the size and resolution. Type in **4 x 4** in the dimensions and choose **150** for the resolution. Keep the options for **Outline patches and blocks** checked. Click **OK**.

Drawing a Sweet Gum Leaf Block

Companion Book Three   **137**

Chapter 4: Drawing Outside the Box

6. Click **BLOCK > New Block > EasyDraw Block**.

7. On the Precision Bar, enter these values:
   - Block Width = **6.00**
   - Block Height = **6.00**
   - Snaps Horizontal = **96**
   - Snaps Vertical = **96**
   - Graph Paper visibility is toggled **OFF**

8. Click **BLOCK > Import Image for Tracing**. In the Import Image for Tracing dialog, beside where it says *Look in*, navigate to the **My Documents\My EQ6\Images** folder and select the *sweetgumleaf.PNG* that you saved earlier and then click on **Open**.

9. On the Import Image dialog that comes up next, keep the default settings (*Fit image to block size* is selected and *lightness* is set at 50%). Click **OK**.

10. You will see a message next asking you if you want to turn off Auto Fill in PatchDraw, click **No**.

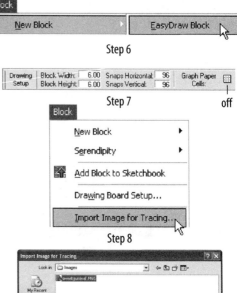

Step 6

Step 7   off

Step 8

Navigate to file and click open

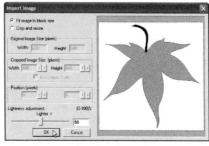

Step 9

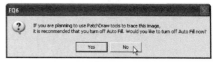

Step 10

Chapter 4: Drawing Outside the Box

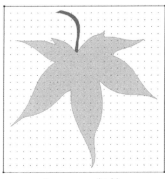

Image on worktable

Step 11

Step 12
Line

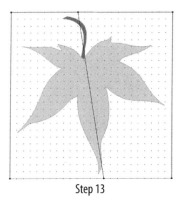

Step 13

11 The image should now be on the worktable and you will see three tabs at the bottom of the screen. You will be on the Image tab when you import the image, so click on the **EasyDraw** tab to switch to the drawing board.

> **Note**
> If you need more help with importing images for tracing see pages 262-264 of the *EQ6 User Manual*.

Now, before you do any drawing, you need to take a good long look at the image. Try to visualize the leaf divided into sections and subsections with only straight seams. It takes practice to be able to see this in your mind, but as you work through the rest of the exercise, it will make more sense to you.

> **Note**
> See the exercise on Drawing a Simple Foundation Pieced House in Chapter 2 on page 76 for more tips about drawing foundation patterns.

12 Click on the **Line** tool.

Remember it's easier to work from the larger to the smaller patches when drawing a foundation pattern. So the first two lines we draw will establish the major sections or units of our foundation block.

After looking over the block, I've decide make the seam lines follow what might be the natural veins of the leaf. This is not the only way to trace this leaf, but it's a good starting point, which in the end, will make the leaf look more realistic.

13 Starting at the top of the block outline, somewhat left of center over the stem, draw a line down through the leaf to the bottom of the block. Before you release the mouse swing the line to the right so that in runs through where the stem meets the leaf and runs downs just to the right of the tip of the leaf. *Be sure to begin and end the line on the block outline.*

Chapter 4: Drawing Outside the Box

Because we have set the snap points at such a high number, it gives us more flexibility for line angles. There is no precise placement for this first line, and your line does not need to be exactly the same as mine. If you are not happy with the angle of the first line, switch to the **Shape** tool and adjust it. Select the line with the **Shape** tool and then grab the end node to move it around. The other node is anchored to the drawing board so you have a lot of wiggle room when moving the other end. If you adjust the line, just make sure that the end nodes attach to the block outline.

> **Note**
> Press the SPACEBAR to toggle between the Line tool and the Shape tool.

14   Draw a second line beginning at the top-left corner of the block down to the right side of the block. The line should come out through the tip of the large lobe on the right and will intersect with the first line near the base of the stem. **Add to Sketchbook**. Now we have established a node at the base of the stem that we can use for the remaining sections of the foundation.

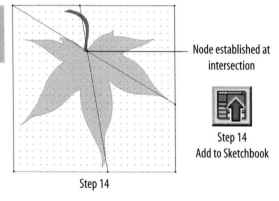

Node established at intersection

Step 14
Add to Sketchbook

Step 14

15   Next draw lines radiating out from the new node at the base of the stem to the block outline, angling them so that they go through the lobes and notches of the leaf. **Add to Sketchbook**.

Now we'll work on one section at a time to finish our foundation pattern. This is where you will learn to simplify. Most of the sections can be done with two or three patches in each section, but the top of the leaf will require a little more detail. Let's start with the easy sections and work our way to the top.

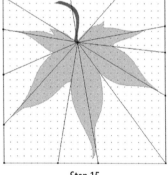

Step 15
Add to Sketchbook

Step 15

140   EQ6 Pieced Drawing

Chapter 4: Drawing Outside the Box

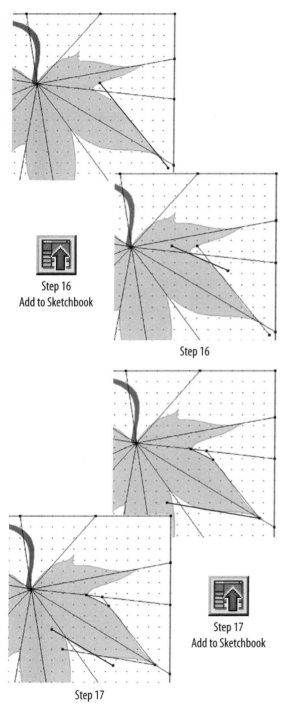

Step 16
Add to Sketchbook

Step 16

Step 17
Add to Sketchbook

Step 17

16   Working on the large lobe on the right, draw a line that follows the top of the lobe and extends beyond the section lines on both ends. It's important that it extends so that it intersects with these lines. Switch to the **Shape** tool if you need to adjust the line. Draw a second shorter line to give the shape to the lobe, again making sure it extends beyond the lines. When both lines are drawn and adjusted, click **Add to Sketchbook**.

Notice that we are using the Line tool with the default snap settings. This is much better for complex foundations because nodes are not established until after you add the block to the Sketchbook, allowing us to adjust lines easily with the Shape tool. You can always increase the snap points if you want even more flexibility for angles. I do not recommend using the Snap to Drawing feature for complex foundations—unless you always draw your lines correctly the first try! Nodes cannot be undone once they are created when drawing with Snap to Drawing turned on, so it actually makes it much harder.

17   Since we established a node at the tip of the lobe in step 16 we can use that to draw the next line. Draw the first line beginning at the node at the tip of the leaf and then draw a shorter one to mimic the curve as before. **Add to Sketchbook**.

It's important to keep adding the foundation pattern to the Sketchbook after you finish a section. Not only can you use the established nodes to draw the next section, but it trims off the line extensions. Saving often will also making it easier to fix any problems you might encounter with your foundation. You can always go back to the last known good step. Let's look at the foundation now to see how we've done so far.

Chapter 4: Drawing Outside the Box

18 Click on the **Print button > Foundation Pattern** (or click FILE > Print > Foundation Pattern). If EQ views your sectioning as okay, the Sections tab will come up first and you should see something like the example if your sectioning is "good." If there is a problem with your foundation (like an inside corner) the Numbering tab will come up first and there will be a message indicating the problem. Click **Close** to exit the print dialog when you're done.

19 Continue drawing the remaining sections one at a time around the leaf in a similar manner (except for the two stem sections). Remember to simplify, share nodes whenever possible and to **Add to Sketchbook** after each section. For the tops of the lobes, you can make them in the same way or add another line or two to create the extra notch. Some sweet gum leaves don't have the notches and some do. Notice how I simplified the bottom lobe of the leaf—I decided I didn't need that extra curve at the tip!

Step 18

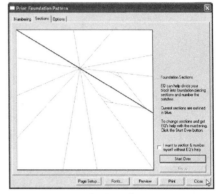

Sections tab

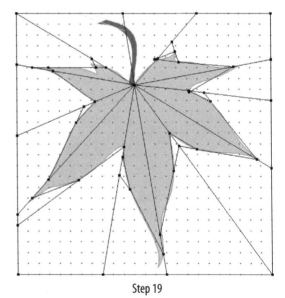

Step 19

Chapter 4: Drawing Outside the Box

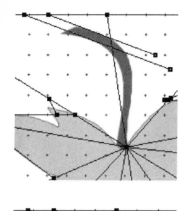

Step 20

Step 20
Add to Sketchbook

20. To draw the stem sections, work on the one on the left first. Draw two lines from the block outline above and below the stem. **Add to Sketchbook**. Draw a line across these to create the end of the stem. If part of your stem is in the lower-right corner of this section, you will also need to draw a line there. **Zoom in** for this one and adjust the line so that it doesn't cross into the next section. If you can't get the angle without crossing that line, you can delete the extra line after adding it to the Sketchbook. Click **Add to Sketchbook**.

> **Note**
> If you want more curve in the stem end, you can draw additional lines—it all depends on how much detail you want.

21. Last section! Start by drawing a line from the block outline down the right side of the stem to the main node at the base of the stem. Draw lines to define the curve. Click **Add to Sketchbook** when you're done.

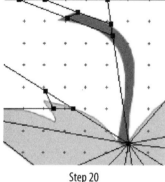

Step 20
Add to Sketchbook

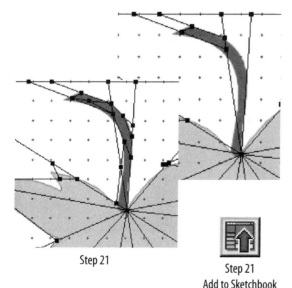

Step 21

Step 21
Add to Sketchbook

Drawing a Sweet Gum Leaf Block

Companion Book Three **143**

Chapter 4: Drawing Outside the Box

22. Click the Color tab and color the block using solid gray (R128, G128, B128) for the leaf and white for the background. **Add to Sketchbook**. Coloring it grayscale first will help when you print the foundation pattern and check the grayscale option. After you save the grayscale coloring you can change the fabrics as you like.

23. Click **FILE > Print > Foundation Pattern** to preview the foundation pattern when you finish. You may need to regroup the sections as I did. I started by grouping each of the stem sections since they have the smaller patches, that way if I made a mistake it would be easier to start over. Remember you can hold down the **SHIFT** key and click on a patch to undo as long as you have not clicked on the **Group** button.

If you love foundation piecing, try some of the other appliqué motif leaves or try importing one of your own photos to trace.

Step 22

Step 22
Add to Sketchbook

Step 22
Grayscale block

Step 23

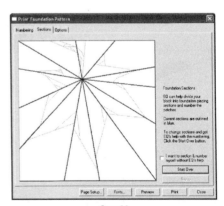
Step 23

Chapter 4: Drawing Outside the Box

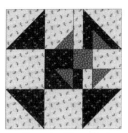

Example of *Inset* Block

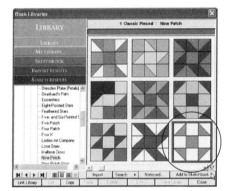

Step 1

Step 2
View Sketchbook

Step 3

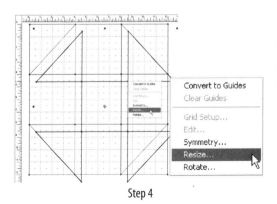

Step 4

Creating an Inset Block

Don't confuse the inset blocks in this exercise with EQ6's Serendipity Merge blocks feature. In this exercise you'll learn how to take a block and make smaller copies of it and add it to the block so that it gives the illusion that they overlap or are set inside the block itself. Part of the challenge comes from having to redraw some of the lines to make piecing easier. Let me show you how.

1   First, add the *Shoo Fly* block from the Block Library to the Sketchbook. Click **LIBRARIES > Block Library.** Then **click EQ6 Libraries > 1 Classic Pieced > Nine Patch.** Select *Shoo Fly*, then click **Add to Sketchbook.** Click **Close.**

2   Click the **View Sketchbook** button and click on **Blocks.** Select the *Shoo Fly* block and click on **Edit** to place it on the worktable.

3   On the Precision Bar, enter these values pressing your keyboard TAB key after each:

- Block Width = **12.00**
- Block Height = **12.00**
- Snaps Horizontal = **24**
- Snaps Vertical = **24**
- Graph Paper visibility is toggled **ON**
- Cells Horizontal = **12**
- Cells Vertical = **12**

Note
If you still see the tracing image in the background of your block from the previous lesson, click the Image tab. Right-click on the worktable and choose Delete. Click Yes to delete the image.

4   Select All (**CTRL+A**). Then **copy** (**CTRL+C**) and then **paste** (**CTRL+V**) the block back onto itself. While the copy is still selected, right-click and choose **Resize** from the context menu.

Companion Book Three   **145**

Chapter 4: Drawing Outside the Box

5. On the Resize dialog, change both the horizontal and vertical percent to **50** and click **OK**.

6. While still selected, move the resized *Shoo Fly* up and over to the right so it is 4" from the bottom of the block and 1" from the right side of the block.

7. Click the **Line** tool. Draw additional lines to create seams for easier piecing. You do not have to draw a square around the little *Shoo Fly* inset. There is no set way to draw these seams, but I always keep in mind how I am going to sew the block. Thus, I usually try to draw my seam lines in a way that creates as few seams as possible and so that they can easily be rotary cut.

8. Click **Add to Sketchbook** and then use the **Pick** tool to delete the vertical line in the center of the small *Shoo Fly*.

9. **Add to Sketchbook** again to save your new block.

Don't stop with just one!

- Add more than one inset to a block or resize the copy by 25%, so that it looks like you have several little blocks floating over the original.

- Eliminate the original block by selecting all of it and resizing without copying it. Float several little copies of in the block and then draw the seamlines.

- Try other insets using a different blocks from the library.

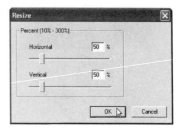
Step 5

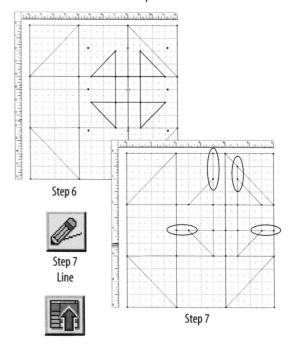
Step 6

Step 7
Line

Step 7

Step 8
Add to Sketchbook

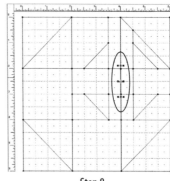
Step 8
Delete vertical line

Step 9
Add to Sketchbook

Chapter 4: Drawing Outside the Box

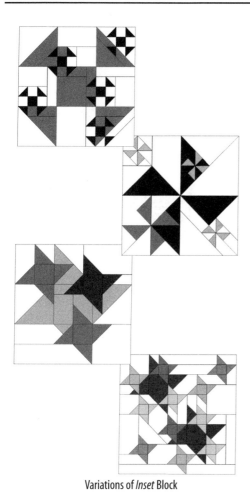

Variations of *Inset* Block

As you experiment more with inset blocks here are some tips that will help:

- Changing the block size is not essential, but it may help you visualize your final block, especially when coloring it with fabrics, as the fabrics will scale according to block size.

- Change graph paper to make placing your inset easier and to aid in drawing additional seam lines.

- Remember to draw additional seam lines after you place your insets!

- I find that this technique works best if I only resize insets 50% or 25%. Double or quadruple the snap points as needed to make the inset snap neatly within the block. Don't try to resize by odd percentages because they will not match up with the grid points.

- Remember to use Copy instead of Clone so that you can easily paste a new block to resize.

- I usually stick with simple, easy to recognize blocks for this inset technique so that piecing will be easier. However, don't be afraid to try experiment with a harder one!

- These inset blocks not only make an intriguing block that can be repeated or rotated in a larger quilt, but they also make wonderful mini quilts by themselves. Imagine them as little custom set quilts. The difference because it's a block, you create the spacer patches in EasyDraw™. The real bonus is you can print rotary cutting directions for them!

Chapter 4: Drawing Outside the Box

Creating an Offset Shadow Block

In this exercise we'll learn how to draw a block that gives the illusion that it has a shadow. The challenging part comes when we have to eliminate and then redraw lines to create the shadow. The effect is well worth the effort! We'll use a familiar block that's easy to draw, the *Sawtooth Star*.

1   Click **WORKTABLE > Work on Block**.

2   Click **BLOCK > New Block > EasyDraw Block**.

3   On the Precision Bar, enter these values pressing your keyboard TAB key after each:

- Block Width = **9.00**
- Block Height = **9.00**
- Snaps Horizontal = **36**
- Snaps Vertical = **36**
- Graph Paper visibility is toggled **ON**
- Cells Horizontal = **9**
- Cells Vertical = **9**

4   Click the **Line** tool. Draw a horizontal and a vertical line on the right side and bottom of the block, 1" from the block outline, creating an offset frame. **Add to Sketchbook**.

5   **Select All (CTRL+A)**, right-click and choose **Convert to Guides**. This sections off an 8" area in the upper-left of the block so that we can easily draw our *Sawtooth Star*.

Example of *Offset Shadow* Block

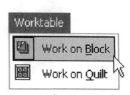

Step 1

Step 2

Step 3

Step 4 Line | Step 4 Add to Sketchbook

Step 4

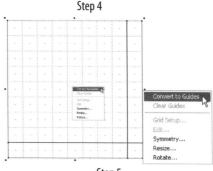

Step 5

148   EQ6 Pieced Drawing

Chapter 4: Drawing Outside the Box

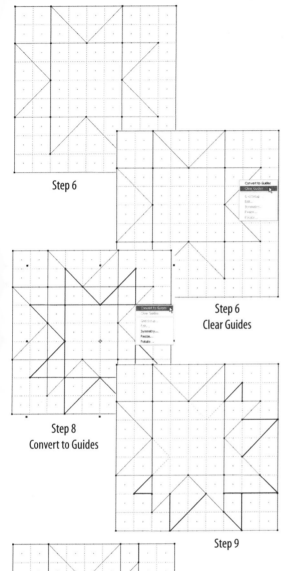

Step 6

Step 6 Clear Guides

Step 8 Convert to Guides

Step 9

Step 11 Add to Sketchbook

Step 10

6   Draw the *Sawtooth Star* within the 8" area we sectioned off with guides, but don't draw lines on the right side or the bottom of the star where the guidelines are, leave these sides open. After you have drawn the star, right-click and choose **Clear Guides**.

7   **Select All (CTRL+A)**, **copy (CTRL+C)** and then **paste (CTRL+V)** the star. Move the copy down to the right so that the points of the star snap to the grid along the right and bottom outline of the block. **Don't add to sketchbook yet!**

8   While the copied block is still selected, right-click and choose **Convert to Guides**.

9   Now draw seam lines to create patches for the shadow. Start by drawing lines wherever you see the guides *outside* the original *Sawtooth Star*. You do not have to draw the lines that would normally be the center square of this offset star—we're creating a shadow, not overlapping block. You might find it helpful to turn off the graph paper lines if you having trouble seeing your guides.

10 To complete the block for easy piecing, draw short lines from the star points to the block outline (upper-right, right side and left and bottom).

11 Click **Add to Sketchbook** when you're done.

Creating an Offset Shadow Block

Companion Book Three   **149**

Chapter 4: Drawing Outside the Box

Helpful Hints for offset shadow blocks:

- Add the amount of the offset you want to use to the size of your original block. For example, for an 8" block, if you want an offset of 1", change the block size to 9.00. If you want a 1/2" offset, make the block size 8.50. You are not limited to these two offsets as you'll see in the variations!

- You will most likely need to change the snap points of the new offset block to be able to draw the original block. If the original block was 8.00 with snap points of 32 x 32 (32/8 = 4), multiply times 4 (9 x 4 = 36) for the new 9.00 offset block. If you're offsetting only 1/2" you would change the snap points in the same way, 8.5 x 4 = 34.

- Graph paper divisions can only be in whole numbers, so double the block size to set your graph paper divisions for odd size blocks.

- Keep your block piecing-friendly. If you plan to foundation piece the block, check the Print Preview after you add your seam lines. Make changes if needed.

- Color tip: Shadow fabric colors should be a darker value of the background fabric, not the main block fabric. A mottled black or dark gray usually works well if you want to make the main block really stand out from the quilt.

- When you set shadow blocks in a quilt layout, keep the shadows all going one direction—unless your quilt has more than one light source!

- To preview what your shadow block will look like without the black outlines (after you have colored the block, place it in a quilt layout, right-click on the quilt and uncheck Outline patches.

Of course you'll want to try other shadow blocks! Here are three you can try at the top of this page.

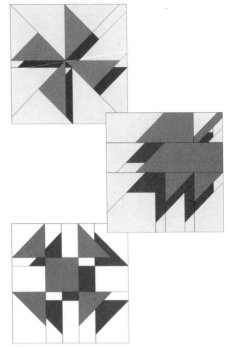

Variations of *Offset Shadow* Block

Challenge
Try an offset block that looks transparent! Don't convert the block to guides after pasting (step#7), instead keep all the lines. Color the block as if the colors are transparent and overlapping. Here is a *Shoo Fly* block I drew, shown with and without the black outlines. (Hint: Offset block size is 14" x 14", draw the main block as 12" x 12")

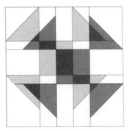

Block with patches outlined

Block without patches outlined

Chapter 4: Drawing Outside the Box

Example of block created using *Node Select All* option

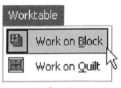

Step 1

Step 2

Step 3

Step 4

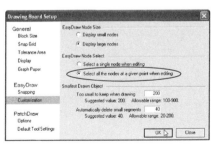

Step 4

Exercising with Node Select All

An often overlooked option in EQ6 is a feature that allows us to select a node with the Shape tool and all line or curve segments that are connected to the node will also be selected. This option is referred to as *Node Select All*. This exercise will show how you can make use of this feature for some really cool effects in EasyDraw™.

1   Click **WORKTABLE > Work on Block**.

2   Click **BLOCK > New Block > EasyDraw Block**.

3   On the Precision Bar, enter these values pressing the TAB key after each:

  - Block Width = **6.00**
  - Block Height = **6.00**
  - Snaps Horizontal = **24**
  - Snaps Vertical = **24**
  - Graph Paper visibility is toggled **ON**
  - Cells Horizontal = **6**
  - Cells Vertical = **6**

4   Click **BLOCK > Drawing Board Setup > EasyDraw Customization**. Under **EasyDraw Node Select**, choose *Select all nodes at a given point when editing* > OK.

Companion Book Three   **151**

Chapter 4: Drawing Outside the Box

5   Click on the **Arc** tool. Starting at the top-center of the block, draw four arcs to make a circle that fills the block.

6   Click on the **small red square** on the **Shape** tool, bringing up the Edit Arc box. Click on each arc separately and on the Edit Arc box, click on **Thirds** for each arc.

7   Click on the **Arc** tool. Draw twelve arcs from the nodes on the circle to the center of the block, having them all facing the same direction. **Add to Sketchbook**.

Now the fun begins!

8   Click on the **Shape** tool and click on the node in the center. Notice that all of the arcs are selected too. Now, drag the node to another grid point within the circle and all of the arcs will move with it. **Add to Sketchbook**.

Note that the node you are moving around is still affected by Snap to grid. You can turn off Snap to Grid and make the center of your swirl anywhere you like, but don't get too carried away—all of the arcs should stay within the circle and don't allow the arcs to bend so much that they cross back over each other.

Try other circle blocks with converging lines or arcs. Partition all the inner arcs and draw additional lines or make them into geese curves!

Note
You can still select individual line or arc segments and move them independently, by clicking on the segment first and then moving the node.

Variations of blocks created using the *Node Select All* option

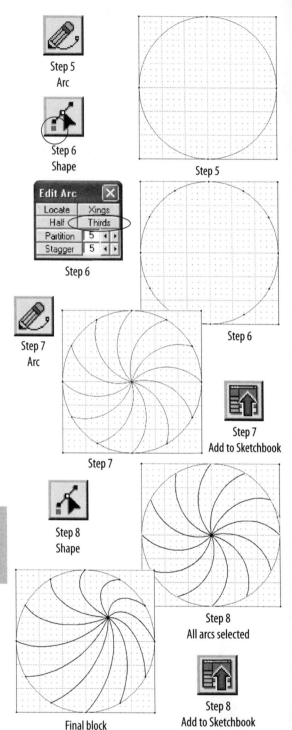

152   EQ6 Pieced Drawing

Chapter 4: Drawing Outside the Box

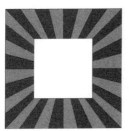

Example of *Perspective Window Frame* Block

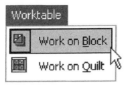

Step 1

Step 2

Step 3

Creating a Perspective Window Frame Block

Here's a really cool window frame-type block that has lots of potential. The angles of the lines converge to a vanishing point giving it the illusion of depth. It looks great around landscape quilts, floral appliqué or even a photo image.

1. Click **WORKTABLE > Work on Block**.

2. Click **BLOCK > New Block > EasyDraw Block**.

3. On the Precision Bar, enter these values pressing the TAB key after each:

    - Block Width = **8.00**
    - Block Height = **8.00**
    - Snaps Horizontal = **32**
    - Snaps Vertical = **32**
    - Graph Paper visibility is toggled **ON**
    - Cells Horizontal = **8**
    - Cells Vertical = **8**

4. Click on the **Line** tool. Draw lines spaced 1" apart from the block outline to the center point of the block. **Add to Sketchbook**. The center will look thick and dark even though there is only one node.

Now we're going to cut a window out of our block.

5. Following the graph paper lines, draw a 4" square in the center of the block 2" in from the block outline (two graph paper squares). **Add to Sketchbook** to establish nodes.

6. Click the **Pick** tool and delete all the converging lines within the center square. Hold down the **DELETE** key and click to make quick work of deleting all these lines. **Add to Sketchbook.**

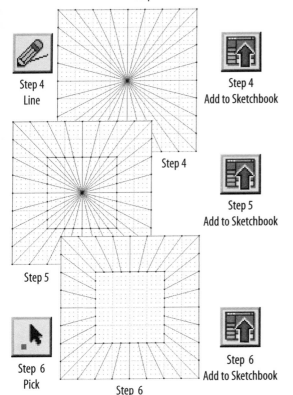

Companion Book Three **153**

Chapter 4: Drawing Outside the Box

At the end of this exercise, I'll show you some ways you can use this block. But first let's take the converging line block we saved in step 4 and give our window a different point of view.

7   Retrieve the block from the Sketchbook that was saved in step 4 and place it on the worktable.

8   Click on the **Shape** tool. Click on the node in the center of the block and drag it up to the graph paper intersection at 6" horizontal and 2" vertical.

With the Node Select All feature turned on, we changed the horizon line and the vanishing point in one easy step!

> **Note**
> If you haven't done the *Exercising with Node Select All* lesson, do step 4 on page 151 now to ensure that the Node Select All option is turned on.

9   Click on the **Line** tool. To create a cutout for a frame, draw a 4 x 4 square around the vanishing point. Top and right side of the square are 1" in from the block outline. Look for where the lines that stem from the block corners cross the graph paper intersections. **Add to Sketchbook** to establish nodes.

10 With the **Pick** tool, delete all the lines within the square. **Add your finished block to the Sketchbook**.

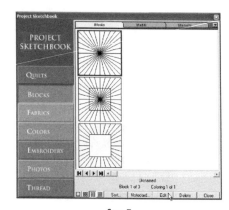
Step 7

Step 8
Shape

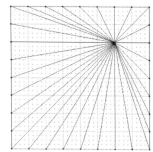
Step 8

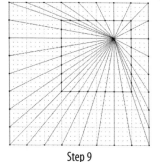
Step 9

Step 9
Line

Step 9
Add to Sketchbook

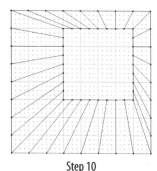
Step 10

Step 10
Pick

Step 10
Add to Sketchbook

Perspective Window Frame

Chapter 4: Drawing Outside the Box

Other Ideas for Perspective Frames

You can also draw rectangle window frames, but you will need to experiment with block size and the divisions if you want to keep a frame effect. Alternatively, you can resize your square block into a rectangle in the quilt layout.

You can divide the perspective frame by drawing additional lines to create a grid. To do this, partition the lines stemming from the block corners and then connect the nodes with lines around the frame. If you want the grid to become smaller as it goes towards the center, increase the snap points and gradually space the grid closer together. And if you are really adventurous, you can further partition the perspective grid and draw small quilt blocks within them.

Let's not forget circle and oval windows! They look great around appliqué. You already know how to create a circle with four arcs. To create an oval, draw four arcs just as you would for a circle, but make parallel sides closer together. When you first draw the arcs of your oval it will look lopsided. To make a nice smooth oval, use the Shape tool, select the arcs and adjust the tent handle so that it makes a right angle from the nodes. The drawing board illustration shows an oval without the converging lines so you can see how to adjust the handles.

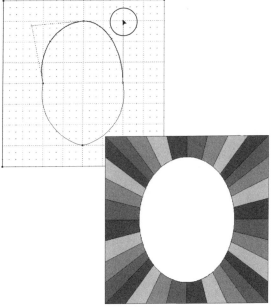

Variations of *Perspective Frame* Blocks

Companion Book Three

Chapter 4: Drawing Outside the Box

Using the Window Block

On the Block worktable you can use the cutout frame blocks with Serendipity > Merge Blocks. Use blocks from the Library or create your own to merge into the frame.

On the Quilt worktable, set the window frame block in a 1 x 1 Horizontal quilt layout or place it on Layer 1 of a Custom Set layout. Custom Set will give you more flexibility and you can easily change the proportions of the block. Once you've set it in the quilt, switch to Layer 2 and place a block or an imported picture over the window opening, adjusting the size to fit the window.

To make a window frame block look even more three dimensional, add a block style border with matching block divisions. On Layer 2 place appliqué motifs or blocks in varying sizes to make it look like your quilt has depth. By the way…the rooster and the cool cats are in the Block Library under Contemporary Appliqué.

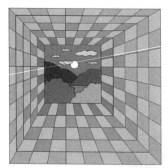
Merged block

Motif on Layer 2

Photo on Layer 2

Merged block, motifs on Layer 2 with a block style border

Chapter 4: Drawing Outside the Box

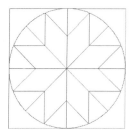 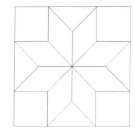

Examples of *LeMoyne Star* Block

Step 1

Eight Slices of a Circle

The eight-point star goes by many names, but most quilters know it as the *LeMoyne Star*. Learning about how the *LeMoyne Star* is drawn is important to add to your EQ drawing skills, because countless blocks are based on this star.

Just a Little Math

The *LeMoyne Star*, as well as many blocks that are derived from it, fall into the category of quilt blocks that are based on eight equal slices of a circle. A circle has 360 degrees, so if you drew a circle and divided it into eight equal slices, each slice would have an angle of 45 degrees (360 ÷ 8 = 45). The *LeMoyne Star* is made up of "true" 45 degree diamonds, meaning that the diamonds have four equal sides and two pairs of parallel sides. So how do we draw a circle-based block in EasyDraw™? Let's copy the *LeMoyne Star* from the Block Library and take a closer look at it and see if we can figure it out.

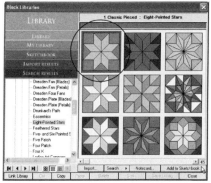

Step 1

Step 2
View Sketchbook

1. Click **LIBRARIES > Block Library > EQ6 Libraries.** Under **1 Classic Pieced: Eight-Pointed Stars,** find the *LeMoyne Star*. It's the first one in that category. Select it and click **Add to Sketchbook**. **Close** the Block Library.

2. Open the **Sketchbook > Blocks section**, select the *LeMoyne Star* and click **Edit** to place it on the worktable.

3. On the Precision Bar the block size should be **24.00 x 24.00** snaps should be **24 x 24** and the graph paper divisions should be **24 x 24**. If they are not, go ahead and change them now. Make sure also that the graph paper lines are showing.

Step 2

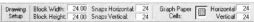

Step 3

Companion Book Three   **157**

Chapter 4: Drawing Outside the Box

The block to the right was drawn on a 24 x 24 grid. Look at the top edge of the *LeMoyne Star*. Counting left to right, there are **7" to the first star point, 10" between the star points and then 7" from the second star point to the right side of the block**. Since **7 + 10 + 7 = 24**, then that's the formula we need to draw the block in EasyDraw™!

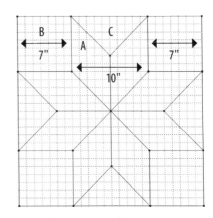

The 7-10-7 formula is based on a geometry principle known as Pythagorean Theorem. If you don't know geometry, don't worry about it! Let me give you the numbers you'll need to translate this into a quilt block you can draw in EasyDraw™ and a block you can sew when you've made your pattern.

Look at the block again. Notice that the sides of the diamond patch **A** are equal to the sides of the corner square **B** and the short sides of the triangle **C**. The long edge of triangle **C** is the same length of the diagonal of square **B**. This size relationship is part of the key to using the 7-10-7 formula and for calculating a finished size for your block, with a goal of making it ruler-friendly.

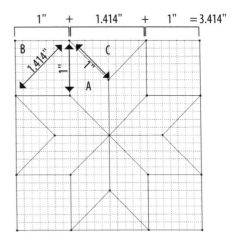

According to Pythagorean Theorem, the diagonal of a square is 1.414 times its side measurement. Apply that to the *LeMoyne Star*. If the sides of the square and diamond measure 1" then that means that the long side of triangle **C** is also 1.414". If we total these measurements for one side of the *LeMoyne Star*, it would be 3.414".

FYI

Here's a little 45 degree math trivia for you. The number 1.414 comes from $a^2 + b^2 = c^2$ (Pythagorean Theorem). In that magic formula, "a" and "b" are the side measurements of the square and "c" is the diagonal measurement of the square. With this formula, if you know any one of the numbers, you can calculate the other two.

Since we know that a and b are equal in a square, we can restate the formula like this: $2a^2 = c^2$. If the side of the square is 1" then it would look like this: $2 = c^2$ (1 squared is 1, and 2 x 1 = 2). So then **c** is the square root of 2. Get your calculator out and find the square root of 2. And the number is…

1.4142135623730950488016887242 09…

The numbers go on to infinity! We quilters usually don't need to work with large numbers like that, so we round it off to three or four decimal points, as that's all we need to figure out the sizes for our patches. Now you know. Just remember that everything I know about geometry I learned as a quilter!

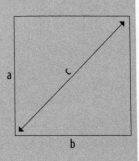

Eight Slices of a Circle

158 EQ6 Pieced Drawing

All that said, those measurements are not usable for setting up our snap points to draw the block in EasyDraw™. We have to find sizes in whole numbers instead. The closest we can come is 7", 10" and 7" whereas 7 + 10 + 7 = 24. The diagonal of a 7" square is 9.898" (7 x 1.414 = 9.898, round up to 10"). That's why we use the 7-10-7 formula in EasyDraw™!

I should mention that drawing a circular based block on a square grid results in an eight-point star that at best is "almost perfect." This does not affect the usability of the block design or its templates.

What size do I make this block?

Now that you know a little bit of the math behind this block, how do we translate that into making an actual block? You can use 7-10-7 formula to calculate sizes for any *LeMoyne*-type block, not just the single eight-point star. So if you forget everything else you've read in the previous section, remember these two things…

- **7 + 10 + 7 = 24** is the formula you'll need for setting up the drawing board in EasyDraw™.

- **1" + 1.414 + 1" = 3.414"** is the formula for calculating sizes for your patterns so that you can actually rotary cut and sew them!

Let's look at how this second formula works.

1   We can start with a known finished block size and use it to determine the size of the patches.

- ***Block size ÷ 3.414 = Side length of the square*** (Remember that the side length of the square is equal to the side length of the diamond and triangle).

For example, if we want our block to be 12":
12.00 ÷ 3.414 = 3.5149, round off to 3.50.

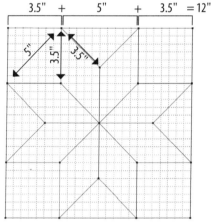

Use block size to calculate patch size

Chapter 4: Drawing Outside the Box

2. We can start also start with the side length of the square, diamond or triangle patch and determine the size of the finished block.

- **Side length of square x 3.414 = Block size**

For example, let's say we want our diamonds and squares to have 3" sides. What would our block size be?
3 x 3.414 = 10.242 (round to 10.25)

For rotary cutting, I would almost always decide on a patch size first, so I could avoid odd decimals which do not translate well on my ruler. For instance, it's much easier to rotary cut pieces for a 10¼" *LeMoyne Star* block than it would be for a 10" block. Of course, if you are determined to have a particular size you can always just print the templates and use them to cut your patches from fabric.

> **Note**
> For quick and easy drawing of single *LeMoyne Star*-type blocks you might want to try the special Pieced PatchDraw Eight Point Star grid. See the exercise on page 39.

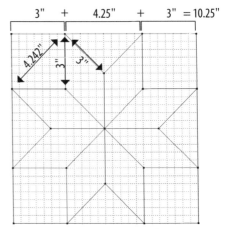

Use patch size to calculate block size

Chapter 4: Drawing Outside the Box

Example of *Rolling Stone* Block

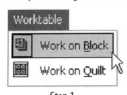

Step 1

Step 2

Step 3

Step 4
Line

Drawing a Rolling Stone Block

This block is in EQ6's Block Library but learning to draw it from scratch will teach you some of the skills you will need to draw many other *LeMoyne*-type stars. You'll also learn how to create an eight-point star by connecting the dots!

1   Click **WORKTABLE > Work on Block**.

2   Click **BLOCK > New Block > EasyDraw Block**.

3   On the Precision Bar, enter these values pressing your keyboard TAB key after each:

- Block Width = **24.00**
- Block Height = **24.00**
- Snaps Horizontal = **24**
- Snaps Vertical = **24**
- Graph Paper visibility is toggled **ON**
- Cells Horizontal = **24**
- Cells Vertical = **24**

4   With the **Line** tool, draw a horizontal and vertical line (at 12") to divide the block into a four-patch. When you've drawn them, select both lines, right-click and choose **Convert to Guides**. This will help us locate the center of the block more easily.

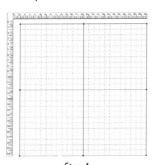

Step 4
Draw lines dividing the block into a four-patch

Step 4
Select lines and Convert to Guides

Companion Book Three   **161**

Chapter 4: Drawing Outside the Box

5 Draw a diagonal line (45 degrees) in each corner, 7" in from the corners in both directions (remember the 7-10-7 rule—count seven graph paper divisions). **Add to Sketchbook** after you have drawn all four diagonals. We now have an octagon to work with.

6 Click on the **Shape** tool, clicking on the **small red square** to bring up the Edit Line box. Click on each diagonal line clicking **Half** in the Edit Line box each time.

7 Switch back to the **Line** tool. Using the new nodes created on the corner diagonals, draw a horizontal square inside the block.

8 Next draw an on-point square in the same manner beginning and ending at the center of the sides of the block outline. **Add to Sketchbook**.

Notice how in just a few strokes we have created the frame for our block made up of true diamonds and right triangles. In the center we've established nodes for another octagon. Now how do we draw an eight-point star in that octagon? We can do this by connecting the dots again.

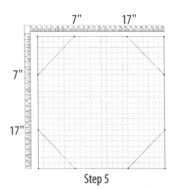
Step 5

Step 6
Shape

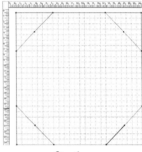
Step 6

Step 6

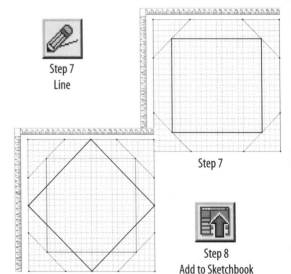
Step 7
Line

Step 7

Step 8

Step 8
Add to Sketchbook

Chapter 4: Drawing Outside the Box

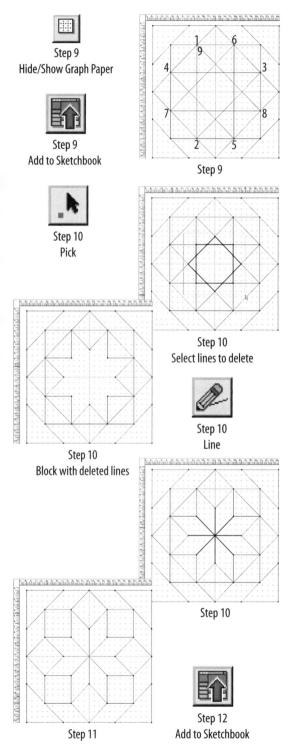

9 First, click on the button on the Precision Bar to hide the graph paper lines. We won't need them to finish this block. Now, draw lines from node to node, following the numbering in the illustration. You should end at the same node in which you began. **Add to Sketchbook** again. This looks like a really nice block at this point, but we need to change the center to make an eight-point star.

10 With the **Pick** tool, drag a marquee to select the center of the star including all the little triangles. Press the **DELETE** key on your keyboard. Now use the **Line** tool to draw lines across the center to complete the diamonds of the eight-point star.

11 To complete the block, select and delete the lines in the squares surrounding the star.

12 **Add to Sketchbook** to save your new *Rolling Stone* block.

Chapter 4: Drawing Outside the Box

Open for Merging...

The frame of diamonds around this block makes a wonderful frame for the star, but you can use it for other blocks too! Retrieve the block that was saved in step 8 from the Sketchbook and place it on the worktable. Delete the corner diagonals to create an open horizontal square in the center of the block. **Add to Sketchbook**. Use this block with the **BLOCK > Serendipity > Merge Blocks** feature in EQ6.

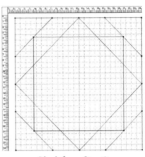
Block from Step 8

Here are four merged blocks that I created. You may need to redraw or delete corner diagonals to get the effect you want. For the last example I merged the merged block twice. It creates a sort of pineapple block effect with diamonds and triangles. Try it and see if you can figure out what I am talking about!

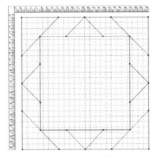
Block with deleted lines

Add to Sketchbook

Variations of blocks merged with *Rolling Stone* frame

Chapter 4: Drawing Outside the Box

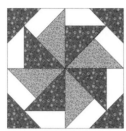

Example of *Eight-Bladed Pinwheel* Block

Step 1

Step 2

Step 3

Step 4
Line

Drawing Eight-Bladed Pinwheels

The first steps to drawing an *Eight-Bladed Pinwheel* starts out similar to the *Rolling Stone* block in the previous exercise. Once we create our basic pinwheel block I'll show you how to make some really neat variations—including a tessellating pinwheel!

1 Click **WORKTABLE > Work on Block**.

2 Click **BLOCK > New Block > EasyDraw Block**.

3 On the Precision Bar, enter these values pressing your keyboard TAB key after each:

  • Block Width = **24.00**

  • Block Height = **24.00**

  • Snaps Horizontal = **24**

  • Snaps Vertical = **24**

  • Graph Paper visibility is toggled **ON**

  • Cells Horizontal = **24**

  • Cells Vertical = **24**

4 With the **Line** tool, draw a horizontal and vertical line (at 12") to divide the block into a four-patch. When you've drawn them, select both lines, right-click and choose **Convert to Guides**. This will help us locate the center of the block more easily.

Step 4
Draw lines dividing the block into a four-patch

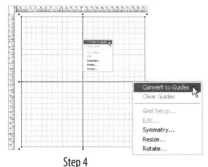

Step 4
Select lines and Convert to Guides

Companion Book Three   **165**

Chapter 4: Drawing Outside the Box

5. Draw a diagonal line (45 degrees) in each corner, 7" in from the corners in both directions. **Add to Sketchbook** after you have drawn all four diagonals.

6. Click on the **Shape** tool, clicking on the **small red square** to bring up the Edit Line box. Click on each diagonal line clicking **Half** in the Edit Line box each time.

7. Switch back to the **Line** tool. Using the new nodes created on the corner diagonals, draw a horizontal square inside the block, then draw an on-point square in the same manner beginning and ending at the center of the sides of the block outline. **Add to Sketchbook**.

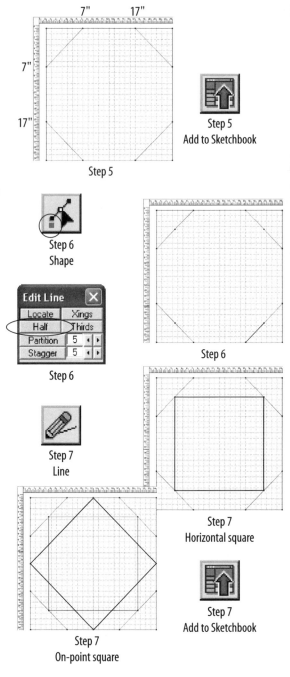

Chapter 4: Drawing Outside the Box

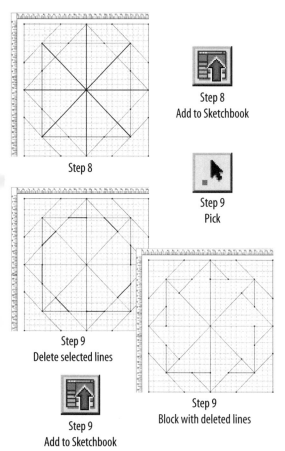

8   Draw two lines from corner to corner in both squares. It should look like the illustration. There will be four lines total. **Add to Sketchbook**.

9   Switch to the **Pick** tool. Starting with the top-left triangle delete the short line segment inside the triangle. Working clockwise, delete the short lines in every other triangle. **Add to Sketchbook**. This is a pinwheel block too! It's sometimes referred to as a *folded pinwheel*. You can color it now if you like so you can easily spot it in the Sketchbook.

10 To finish the basic eight-bladed pinwheel, delete the short lines between the triangular blades around the pinwheel. **Add to Sketchbook** to save the new block.

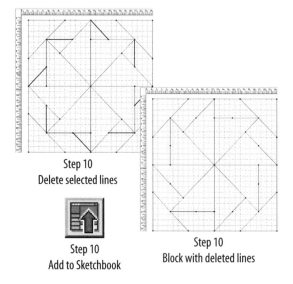

Companion Book Three   **167**

Pinwheel in a Pinwheel

Let's take this block now and make a smaller pinwheel inside the larger one.

11 Retrieve the block from the Sketchbook that was saved in step 8 and place it on the worktable.

12 Using the nodes on the inner octagon, draw another horizontal and on-point square as we did in step 6. **Add to Sketchbook**.

13 Switch to the **Pick** tool. Starting with the top-left triangle of the new small pinwheel, delete the short line segment inside the triangle. Working clockwise, delete the short lines in every other triangle. **Add to Sketchbook**.

There are many variations you can create from the block saved at this stage. Here are a four that I created by just deleting or adding lines. I'm sure you can think of others by now!

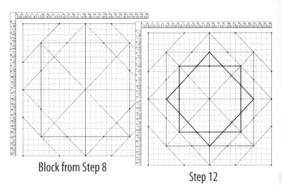

Block from Step 8

Step 12

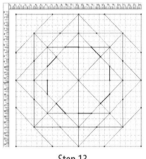

Step 13
Pick

Step 13
Add to Sketchbook

Step 13
Delete selected lines

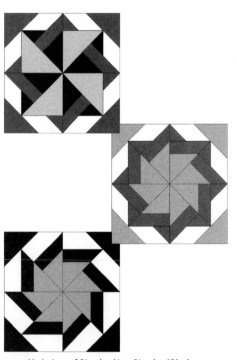

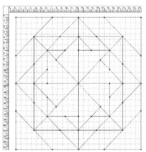

Block with deleted lines

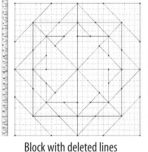

Example of *Pinwheel in a Pinwheel* Block

Variations of *Pinwheel in a Pinwheel* Block

Chapter 4: Drawing Outside the Box

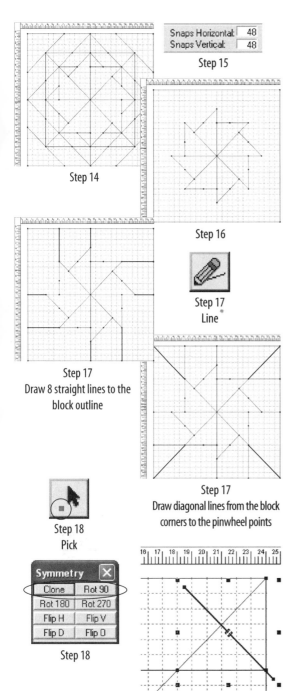

Tessellating Pinwheels

To make our *Tessellating Pinwheel* block, we will have to begin by deleting a lot of lines so that only the smaller pinwheel remains on the block. The result will be worth the challenge!

14 Retrieve the block from the Sketchbook that was saved in step 13.

15 On the Precision Bar, change the snap points to **48 x 48**.

16 Delete all the lines outside the small pinwheel. Don't add this to the Sketchbook yet—we have to anchor it to the block outline first!

17 Switch to the **Line** tool and from each point of the pinwheel draw a straight line out to the block outline (eight lines). Then draw diagonal lines from the corners to the pinwheel points. Now click **Add to Sketchbook**.

To create the tessellation, we have to draw an additional triangle in each of the corners. This is the trickiest part to draw, but I've discovered that we can accomplish this by using clone and rotate.

18 Bring up the Symmetry box by clicking on the **small red square** on the **Pick** tool. Select the diagonal line in the upper-right corner, click **Clone** and then **rotate (Rot 90)**.

Drawing Eight-Bladed Pinwheels

Companion Book Three **169**

Chapter 4: Drawing Outside the Box

19 Move the clone so that the top node is 15½" from the left (or 3½ graph paper squares from top center). The bottom node will be at 21½" (or 2½ squares from the right) and will fall on the horizontal line. You will find it much easier to count the graph paper squares to place the lines.

20 When you are sure the cloned line has snapped into place, *repeat* this process (**Clone** and **Rot 90**) *three times*, moving each successive clone to the next corner. Again, you will find it much easier to count the graph paper squares to place the lines. **Add to Sketchbook**.

21 Now go back and delete the short lines that were created in those first corner blades. **Add to Sketchbook** one more time—done!

Congratulations, you now have a new *Tessellating Pinwheel* block. To get the full effect, place it in a horizontal quilt layout and see what happens. Oh, by the way, you can also use the block from step 17 to make two more repeatable blocks!

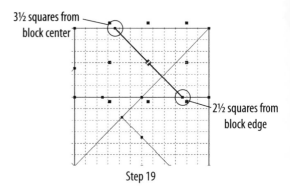
Step 19

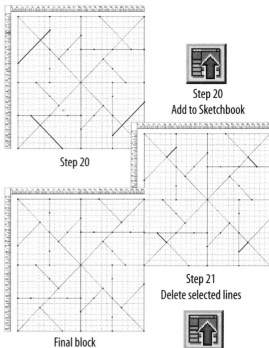
Step 20
Step 20 Add to Sketchbook
Step 21 Delete selected lines
Final block

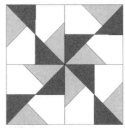
Step 21 Add to Sketchbook

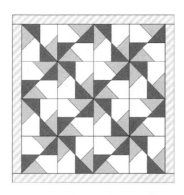

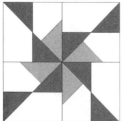 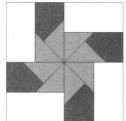
Variations of *Tessellating Pinwheel* Block

Example of *Tessellating Pinwheel* block

Chapter 4: Drawing Outside the Box

Example of *Rising Sun* block

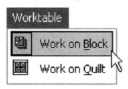

Step 1

Step 2

Step 3

Drawing a Rising Sun Block

This *Rising Sun* block is based on an eight-point grid too, but it's different in that the center octagon is surrounded by half-square triangles. For ease of drawing, we'll set our block size at 44.00 x 44.00, but you'll want to sew it as an 11" block.

1   Click **WORKTABLE > Work on Block**.

2   Click **BLOCK > New Block > EasyDraw Block**.

3   On the Precision Bar, enter these values pressing your keyboard TAB key after each:

- Block Width = **44.00**
- Block Height = **44.00**
- Snaps Horizontal = **44**
- Snaps Vertical = **44**
- Graph Paper visibility is toggled **ON**
- Cells Horizontal = **44**
- Cells Vertical = **44**

4   Click on the **Line** tool and draw a diagonal line (45 degrees) in each corner, 13" in from the corners in both directions. This may seem like an odd measurement, but with the rulers and the graph paper lines showing, you should be able to locate it without any trouble. Zoom in if necessary.

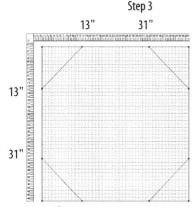

Step 4

> **Helpful Hint**
> Draw one diagonal and then use Clone and Flip on the Symmetry box to create the other three, moving each to its respective corner.

If you find it difficult to see with the graph paper set at 44 x 44, reduce them to 22 x 22. Every square will then represent 2".

5   Draw a diagonal line beginning 7" from the top-left corner and ending at 37" down on the right side of the block (7 squares up from the corner).

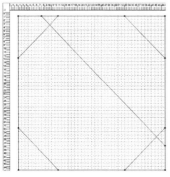

Step 5

Chapter 4: Drawing Outside the Box

6. Switch to the **Pick** tool and click on the **small red square** to bring up the Symmetry box. Select the line you just drew. Click **Clone** and move the cloned line 7" down from the top-left corner.

7. Select both the long diagonals (using the **Pick** tool and **SHIFT** key), **Clone** and **flip horizontal (Flip H)**, placing them so that they snap into place in the opposite direction. **Add to Sketchbook**.

8. Draw two parallel vertical lines down the center of the block. The first one at 17" and the second at 27" (count four squares in from the corner diagonal lines).

Step 6
Pick

Step 6

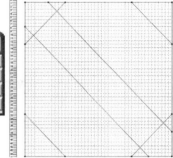
Step 6

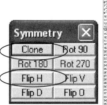
Step 7

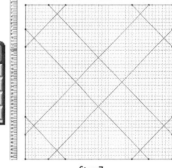
Step 7

Step 7
Add to Sketchbook

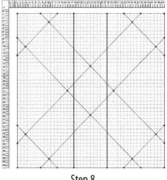
Step 8

Chapter 4: Drawing Outside the Box

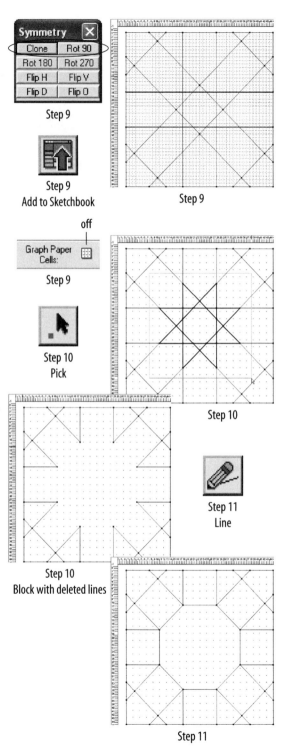

9. **Clone** and **rotate** these lines 90 degrees (**Rot 90**) and move them into place in the center of the block. **Add to Sketchbook**. *Turn off the graph paper.*

10. With the **Pick** tool, drag a marquee around the star that was created in the center and then delete it.

11. With the **Line** tool draw an octagon in the center by connecting the dots around the center. When you do this it also creates squares around the octagon.

Companion Book Three   **173**

Chapter 4: Drawing Outside the Box

12 Draw two lines in each of the squares to create quarter-square triangles. **Add to Sketchbook**.

13 The last thing we need to do is delete the extra lines in each of the corners. Use the **Pick** tool to select and delete the short lines in the corner triangles. **Add to Sketchbook** when you're done to save your new block.

Open for Merging…

I mentioned at the beginning of this exercise that the *Rising Sun* block is traditionally made as an 11" square block. One added bonus to this size is that the center will be 6"—making it a perfect candidate for merging with other blocks.

Delete four of the center diagonal lines to create an open square center. You can make the square horizontal or on-point. **Add this to the Sketchbook** and use it with the **BLOCK > Serendipity > Merge Blocks** feature. You can edit your merged block and redraw the lines if you want to have an octagonal center. While you can merge any block into this square center, be sure to try some eight-point star and kaleidoscope-type blocks—they fit perfectly.

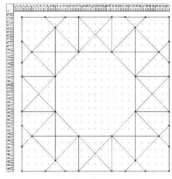

Step 12
Add to Sketchbook

Step 12

Step 13
Pick

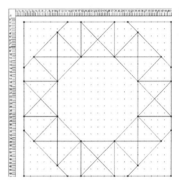

Step 13
Add to Sketchbook

Variations of Merged 7-10-7 Blocks

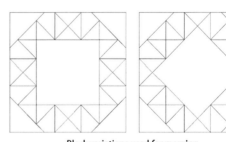

Block variations used for merging

Variations of merged *Rising Sun* blocks

174 EQ6 Pieced Drawing

Chapter 4: Drawing Outside the Box

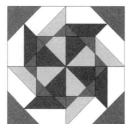
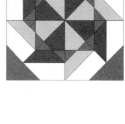

Going Crazy for Eights

This exercise is not about drawing a specific block, but it's all about applying what you have learned. If you have not done the previous exercises on *LeMoyne Star*-type blocks you will need to backtrack to page 157 to read and work through them first.

You can create endless new blocks by drawing smaller eight-point stars, diamonds, pinwheels, kaleidoscopes and octagons inside them. All you need is eight points around a circle or any block based on the 7-10-7 formula. You can use blocks created in the previous exercises or search for blocks in the Block Library under *Eight-Point Stars, Feathered Stars, Kaleidoscopes, Maltese Cross*, etc.

Here are just a few examples you can try. What other blocks can you come up with? Helpful Hint: You may need to partition some lines by half to create new nodes to draw from.

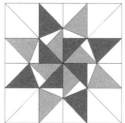

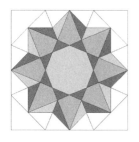

Companion Book Three

Conquering the Radiant Star

This feathered star is my favorite block. I don't think I am alone because it appears in quilts in almost every national and international quilt show and it usually wins a prize. If you draw this block in EasyDraw™ you deserve a prize as well!

I have spent many, many hours playing with it in EQ and trying different ways to accomplish this compass-drawn block on a square grid. I am so excited to share it with you in this exercise!

Example of *Radiant Star* Block

1 Click **WORKTABLE > Work on Block**.

2 Click **BLOCK > New Block > EasyDraw Block**.

Step 1

Step 2

3 On the Precision Bar, enter these values pressing your keyboard TAB key after each:

- Block Width = **41.00**
- Block Height = **41.00**
- Snaps Horizontal = **140**
- Snaps Vertical = **140**
- Graph Paper visibility is toggled **ON**
- Cells Horizontal = **41**
- Cells Vertical = **41**

Step 3

Step 4
Zoom In

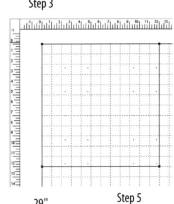

Don't let the large block size and large number of snap points scare you, it's going to make this block very accurate. Because this star block has so many patches, we are using the larger numbers to keep the 45 degree angles as true as possible. Once we get the basic outline of the base eight-point star, we'll switch to a smaller size—the actual size!

4 Use the **Zoom in** tool and zoom in on the top-left corner of the block.

5 Draw a vertical and horizontal line to create a 12" square in the corner. Count twelve squares to the left and twelve squares down. Stay zoomed in and use the scroll bars to move to the remaining three corners and draw a 12" square in each corner.

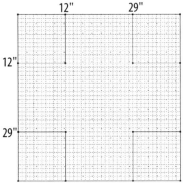

Step 5

Chapter 4: Drawing Outside the Box

Step 6
Zoom Out

Step 6
Add to Sketchbook

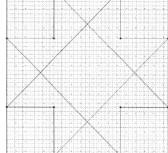

Step 6

Step 7

Step 7
Pick

Step 7
Add to Sketchbook

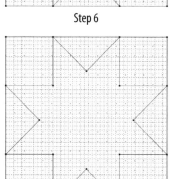

Step 8

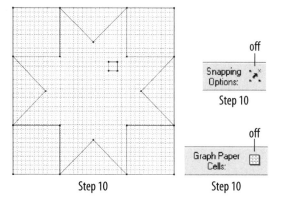

Step 10 · Step 10 · Step 10

6   Zoom out and draw diagonal lines connecting the inside of the star points and creating the side triangles. **Add to Sketchbook**.

7   Select the **Pick** tool. Delete the lines of the on-point square that was created in the center. **Add to Sketchbook**.

Now we're going to change the drawing board to reflect actual size. Our goal for this feathered star is to have 1" feather squares (the small half-square triangles along the star points).

8   On the Precision bar, change the settings as follows:

- Block Width = **18.50**
- Block Height = **18.50**
- Snaps Horizontal = **37**
- Snaps Vertical = **37**
- Graph Paper visibility is toggled **ON**
- Cells Horizontal = **37**
- Cells Vertical = **37**

Note
Two graph paper squares now equals 1".

9   Somewhere in the center of the block, but away from any of the lines already there, draw a 1" square.

10   Turn **OFF** Snap to Grid. The snap to grid option is on the Precision bar and can be toggled on and off. We are turning it off because we only want our square to snap to nodes. *Keep Snap to Grid turned off for the remaining steps.* You can also **turn *off* the graph paper lines now**.

Conquering the Radiant Star

Companion Book Three   **177**

Chapter 4: Drawing Outside the Box

11 Switch to the **Pick** tool and click on the **small red square** to bring up the Symmetry box. Drag a marquee around the 1" square to select it and move it up so that it snaps to the inside corner of the upper-left square patch. Keep it selected and then clone it *three more times* moving each successive square to the next corner node. It's very important that these little squares snap to these corner patch nodes. Zoom in on the center of the block to double-check.

12 **Clone** the square one more time, but this time, right-click while it's selected and choose **Rotate** from the context menu. The degrees of rotation should be at **45 degrees** by default, type it in if it is not, and then click **OK**.

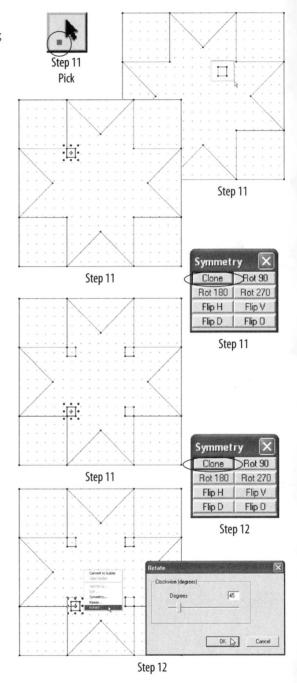

Chapter 4: Drawing Outside the Box

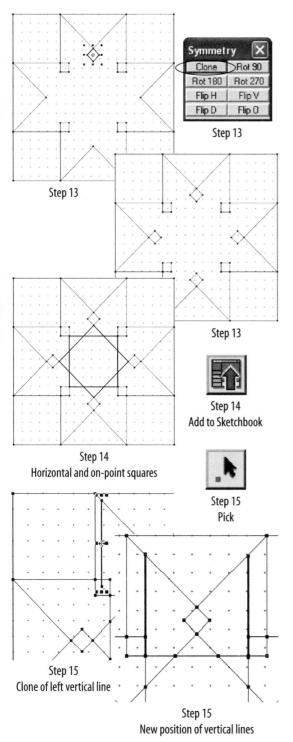

13. Move the rotated square to the inside node of one of the side triangles and then clone it *three more times* snapping one to each triangle. ***Don't Add to Sketchbook yet, we have one more thing to do!***

14. Using the corner nodes of the small squares, draw a horizontal and an on-point square. Now you can **Add to Sketchbook**! The hard part is over now, whew!

15. Working on the top two star points, use the **Pick** tool to **select** and **Clone** the vertical line of the left star point. Move the copied line over 1" and let it snap to side of the 1" square. With the line still selected, click **Clone** again and move the line to the 1" square on the right star point. Let it snap into place.

Companion Book Three   **179**

Chapter 4: Drawing Outside the Box

16 Now **Clone** the 45 degree triangle lines one at a time, moving them down to snap to the small on-point square. These lines will intersect and create a 45 degree diamond at the tip of the star point. It also creates the strip in which we will draw all those little half-square triangles (the feathers). **Add to Sketchbook.**

You could draw all of the star points in this manner, but let's make it easy and clone the rest.

17 Select the lines that create an X in the star points. Hold down the **SHIFT** key on your keyboard and click them one at a time (eight total). Once they're selected, **Clone** and **rotate 90 degrees (Rot 90)** and move them to the star points on the right. When you're attempting to get them to snap into place, aim for the nodes on the small 1" squares. *Repeat* for the remaining pairs of star points and then **Add to Sketchbook**. It should look like the illustration when you're done.

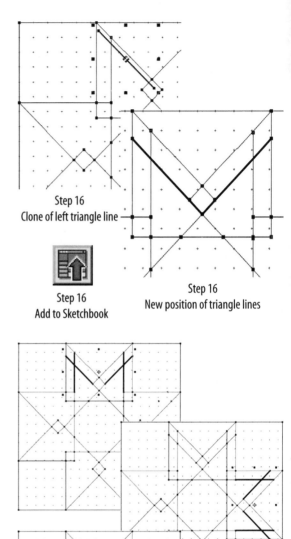

Step 16
Clone of left triangle line

Step 16
Add to Sketchbook

Step 16
New position of triangle lines

Step 17
Add to Sketchbook

Step 17

Chapter 4: Drawing Outside the Box

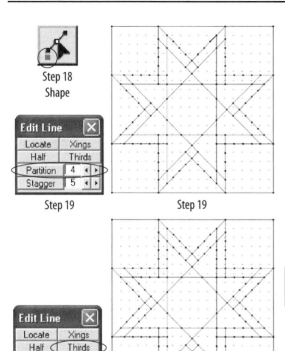

Step 18
Shape

Step 19

Step 19

Step 20

Step 20

Step 21

Step 21
Add to Sketchbook

Step 21

18. To create the squares for the feathers, switch to the **Shape** tool and click on the **small red square** to bring up the Edit Line box.

19. Change the partition number on the Edit Line box to **4**. Click on each of the *outside lines* of the star points then click **Partition**.

20. Once the outside lines are complete, click on *each inside line* of the star points and click **Thirds** on the Edit Line box.

21. Draw lines from node to node across the small squares and then in each square draw lines to divide each square in half, creating the feathers. When you're finished, **Add to Sketchbook**.

IMPORTANT
Turn Snap to Grid back on when you've finished your block!

Congratulations! You've just created a very complex block that usually had to be drawn with a compass. Take a moment now and look over your handiwork on the print preview for rotary cutting directions. Be sure to type in 18.50 for the block size and check the option for large key block so you can see the patch lettering. I like to view the rotary cutting directions because it can tell me if I have kept my angles consistent (or not).

Companion Book Three

Chapter 4: Drawing Outside the Box

Drawing 60° Blocks

In this exercise and the remaining exercises of this chapter we'll concentrate on drawing 60° blocks. Drawing 60° blocks in EasyDraw™ at first may seem daunting, but after I reveal my special drawing method you will see how easy it can be!

Understanding 60° Shapes

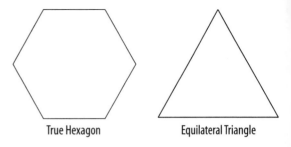

True Hexagon   Equilateral Triangle

There are two basic shapes that quilters use most often for 60° based blocks, a true hexagon and the equilateral triangle. All sides and angles of the hexagon are equal and the same goes for the equilateral triangle. To draw these shapes in EasyDraw™ there are three basic properties we need to keep in mind:

1) The ratio of a hexagon from its shortest measurement (flat side to flat side) to its longest measurement (point to point) is 1 to 1.155.

2) The distance between two points of a hexagon is *twice* the length of its sides.

3) The width to height ratio of an equilateral triangle is 1.155 to 1.

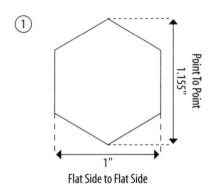

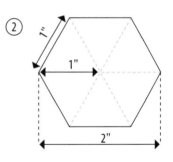

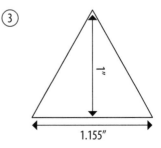

Chapter 4: Drawing Outside the Box

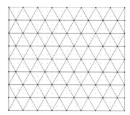

Example of Isometric Guideline

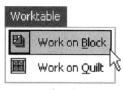

Step 1

Step 2

Creating Isometric Guidelines

The first challenge to drawing 60° blocks in EasyDraw™ is to keep their proper proportions. In order to accomplish this we need to set up the drawing board to match the proportions. We can do that by using the ratio of 1 to 1.155 to size our block. The second challenge is figuring out a way to draw the patches easily—we can do that by creating isometric guidelines. Let's make a block now so you can see this in action. As we work through these first steps I'll insert explanations so that you'll be able to apply it to future blocks.

1   Click **WORKTABLE > Work on Block**.

2   Click **BLOCK > New Block > EasyDraw Block**.

3   On the Precision Bar, enter these values pressing your keyboard TAB key after each:

- Block Width = **8.00**
- Block Height = **6.93***
- Snaps Horizontal = **48**
- Snaps Vertical = **48**
- Graph Paper visibility is toggled **ON**
- Cells Horizontal = **8**
- Cells Vertical = **8**

*Yes, that number 6.93 is correct! You may never have worked with sizes like this before, but in order to create a hexagonal block, you will need to use them. I used the ratio 1 to 1.155 to calculate the block size. If the longest dimension (point to point) of the hexagon is 8" divide by 1.155 to find the shortest measurement (flat side to flat side).

8 ÷ 1.155 = 6.9264 (round up to 6.93)

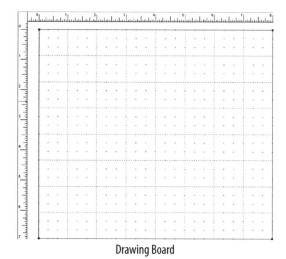

Step 3

Drawing Board

Our block dimensions are now proportioned to those of a horizontal hexagon. This will become more apparent when we complete our isometric guidelines.

Companion Book Three   **183**

Chapter 4: Drawing Outside the Box

> **Note**
> When you create hexagonal blocks, keep the point to point measurement the ruler-friendly number so that the side length will also be ruler friendly. Most traditional hexagonal blocks made up of various 60° shapes have side lengths that match. It will also make it easier to rotary cut the patches.

4   With the **Line** tool, draw a line from the top-left corner of the block to the bottom-center at 4" from the left. Continue drawing left-slanting diagonals spacing them 1" apart. They will get shorter as you go toward the corners. Note how the lines cross at intersections on the graph paper. This is a good way to double-check to make sure your lines are angled correctly and will help you when you need to draw other grids. By the way, due to our block's proportions the angle of these lines is 60°. **Add to Sketchbook**.

5   When you've drawn all the lines, select the **Pick** tool and click on the **small red square** to bring up the Symmetry box. **Select All (CTRL+A)** and **Clone** the lines and **flip horizontally (Flip H)**. Move the clones so that they are centered in the block and snap into place. When you do this you'll have a neat grid of 60° diamonds. **Add to Sketchbook**.

6   Click the **Line** tool. To complete the isometric grid, draw horizontal lines across the block dividing the diamonds in half, creating a grid of equilateral triangles. Now, click **Add to Sketchbook**.

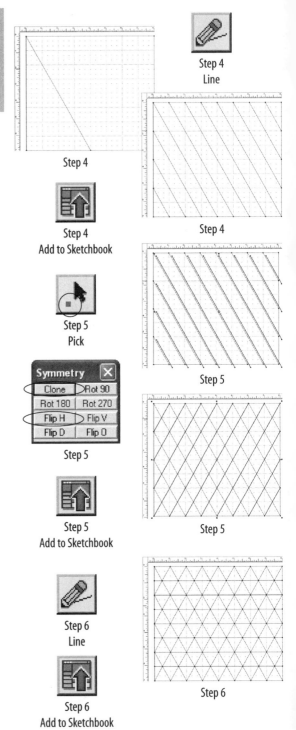

Chapter 4: Drawing Outside the Box

Step 7
View Sketchbook

Step 7

7   When you have saved the block, click **View Sketchbook > Blocks**. Select the block, then click **Notecard** and name the block, ***ED Isometric Grid_Base 4_Horiz*** (ED = EasyDraw) or something similar. Click the "x" in the top-right corner to close the Notecard box, then click **Close**. You will be using this block again, so you want to be able to identify and find it easily. The base number refers to the number of triangles that fit along the sides of the hexagon. Think of it as the hexagon's grid.

Now that your block is saved let me show how this block can help you draw a hexagonal block.

8   With your isometric grid block on the worktable, **Select All (CTRL+A)**, right-click and choose **Convert to Guides**. *Turn off the graph paper visibility.* Now you have guidelines to draw your 60° block!

> **Note**
> You may want to change the color of the guides to make them less distracting. When I'm using the guides like this, I like to change the color to light gray and have the grid dots small. To change the color go to the BLOCK > Drawing Board Setup or click on More Drawing Board Options button on the Precision Bar. Select Display, and under Guide Color click the down arrow to choose a different color. To change the grid dot size, select Snap Grid and check Display small grid dots.

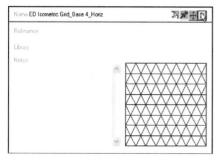
Step 7

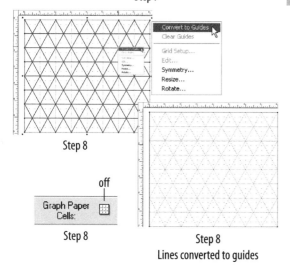
Step 8

Step 8

Step 8
Lines converted to guides

Companion Book Three   **185**

Chapter 4: Drawing Outside the Box

9. Let's start by drawing a full-size basic hexagon star. With our new isometric grid this will be easy! Click on the **Line** tool. Beginning 2" from the top-left, draw a line down to the left-center of the block and then draw a second line from the center down to the bottom 2" from the left. Draw the other side of the hexagon on opposite side of the block. **Add to Sketchbook**.

10. Follow the guides to draw an upright equilateral triangle inside the hexagon. The top point is at the top-center, the bottom points end on the opposite sides of the hexagon. Draw a second triangle in the same manner, but draw it upside down. **Add to Sketchbook**.

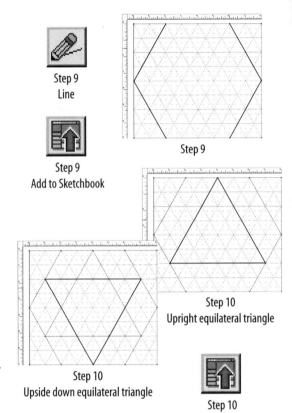

Step 9
Line

Step 9
Add to Sketchbook

Step 9

Step 10
Upright equilateral triangle

Step 10
Upside down equilateral triangle

Step 10
Add to Sketchbook

Now you see how easy it is to draw a hexagon star with our special isometric guidelines. There's no guesswork involved now since our block proportion is set up for 60°—there's a grid point at every intersection of our special grid!

Our Base-4 isometric grid works well for many traditional hexagonal blocks, but just like rectangular blocks, some 60° blocks will require a different grid. In the next section I'll show you four grids (including the Base-4) that you will use most often for 60° blocks. I recommend you draw these grids now and add them in My Library. We will definitely be using them in the following exercises.

> **Notes**
> - For about adding blocks to My Library, see pages 12 and 13 of this book or 143-146 of the *EQ6 User Manual*.
> - To remove guides, right-click on the worktable and choose Clear Guides.

Isometric Grids for 60° Blocks

When drawing these grids, always start with a diagonal line like we did in step 4 of page 184. Continue to draw diagonal lines, then **Select All (CTRL+A)**, **Clone** and **Flip H**. Move the clone into place. Finally, draw the horizontal or vertical lines as indicated in the illustrations.

ED Isometric Grid_Base 4_Horiz
- Block Size: 8.00 x 6.93
- Snaps: 48 x 48
- Graph paper: 8 x 8
- Uses: Horizontal hexagons, stars and triangles.

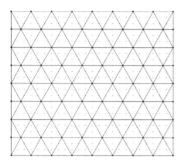
ED Isometric Grid_Base 4_Horiz

ED Isometric Grid_Base 6_Vert
- Block Size: 5.19 x 6.00
- Snaps: 24 x 24
- Graph paper: 12 x 12
- Uses: Vertical hexagons, stars, 3-D cubes, tessellations

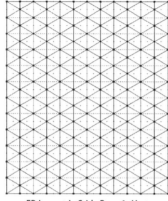
ED Isometric Grid_Base 6_Vert

ED Isometric Grid_Base 3_Horiz
- Block Size: 6.00 x 5.19
- Snaps: 24 x 24
- Graph paper: 12 x 12
- Uses: Horizontal hexagons, stars

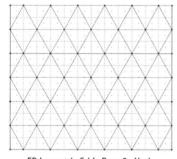
ED Isometric Grid_Base 3_Horiz

ED Isometric Grid_Base 5_Horiz
- Block Size: 10.00 x 8.66
- Snaps: 20 x 20
- Graph paper: 10 x 10
- Uses: Seven Sisters, hexagonal log cabins

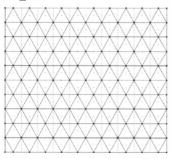
ED Isometric Grid_Base 5_Horiz

> **Note**
> Guides will not save when you exit a project file. If you need to use them again when reopening a project, place the isometric grid block on the worktable first and Convert to Guides.

Chapter 4: Drawing Outside the Box

Drawing Hexagonal Stars

Drawing hexagonal stars is as easy as following the lines of your new isometric grids. If you have not created these grids yet, please go back to the previous exercise and do so now. You will need the *horizontal Base-4 grid* for this exercise.

1. If you are beginning a new project file for this exercise, you will need **horizontal Base-4 grid (ED Isometric Grid_Base 4_Horiz)** to draw these hexagon star blocks. If you saved it in your My Library, go there now and add the grid block to the Sketchbook. Alternatively, you can import it from the original project file.

2. Once you have added the grid block to your Sketchbook, retrieve it and place it on the worktable. Double-check that the settings on the Precision Bar are correct:

   - Block Width = **8.00**
   - Block Height = **6.93**
   - Snaps Horizontal = **48**
   - Snaps Vertical = **48**
   - Graph Paper visibility is turned **OFF**

3. Right-click and choose **Clear Guides** to remove any guides that might be currently visible. Then, **Select All (CTRL+A)**, right-click and choose **Convert to Guides**.

4. Using the **Line** tool, draw a full size horizontal hexagon that fills the block. Then draw two large equilateral triangles, one upright and one upside down. Points of the triangles are at the centers of the sides of the hexagon. **Add to Sketchbook**.

Example of *Hexagonal Star* block

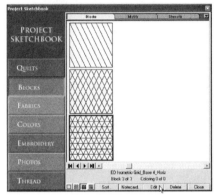

Step 1

Step 2

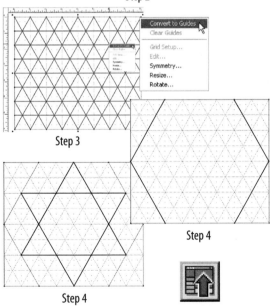

Step 3

Step 4

Step 4

Step 4
Add to Sketchbook

188 EQ6 Pieced Drawing

Chapter 4: Drawing Outside the Box

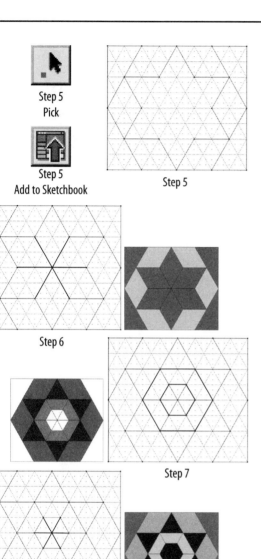

Step 5 Pick

Step 5 Add to Sketchbook

Step 5

Step 6

Step 7

Step 8 Select lines to delete

Step 9 Select lines to delete

5   With the **Pick** tool **select** and **delete** the lines between the star points so that you have an open star in the center. **Add to Sketchbook**.

This will be our base block for several hexagon stars. I'll show you how to do five hexagon stars by simply melding one block into the next and then I'll present you with several stars you can try on your own.

6   Start by drawing lines across the center from node to node creating a simple six-point star. **Add to Sketchbook**.

7   Redraw the lines you deleted in step 5 and then draw a small hexagon around the center. **Add to Sketchbook**.

8   Delete the lines inside the small hexagon. **Add to Sketchbook**.

9   Delete the lines that you redrew in step 7. **Add to Sketchbook**.

You can see how easy these are to draw with our special isometric grid! Now it's your turn to try these hexagon stars. I've set them in a quilt and have included the first five stars we created in this exercise. There are 17 hexagon star blocks. *NOTE: For the last three blocks you will need to use the Base 3 Grid (ED Isometric_Base 3_Horiz).*

Chapter 4: Drawing Outside the Box

BONUS

Make a sampler quilt of your hexagon stars! I used the Horizontal Strip quilt layout for this one. I've alternated the rows between the Half Drop Blocks and Pieced Blocks styles. This creates a secondary star around some of the blocks. If you want to make this quilt, piece the points of these secondary stars as one-piece triangles. You can calculate the size of the triangles easily since you'll already know the length of hexagon sides (4").

Here are the settings I used for the sampler quilt:

- Layout: **Horizontal strip quilt**

- Block Size: **8.00 x 6.94***
  * 6.94 is as close as we can get to the actual height of the block in a quilt layout. Due to the odd size of the hexagon block, you will need to change the nudge settings to get this number. While on the Quilt worktable, click **QUILT > Options > Snap Settings.** Under **Nudge Settings** change the *Palette slider increments* to **1/32**.

- Number of strips: **5**
  I used 17 hexagon star blocks and set a plain block on the ends of the half drop strips.

- Strip styles: Going from top to bottom alternate between **Half Drop Blocks** and **Pieced Blocks** styles.

- Strip width: **6.94**

- Strip length: **32.00**

- Number of blocks along length: **4**

Sampler quilt

Variations of *Hexagonal Star* Blocks

190   EQ6 Pieced Drawing

Chapter 4: Drawing Outside the Box

Variations of *Hexagonal Star* Blocks

Notes
- If you need more help with Strip Quilt layouts see pages 154-158 of the *EQ6 User Manual*.

- When you use your 60 ° blocks in a quilt layout, be sure to keep the block size as close as possible to the 1 to 1.155 ratio. In order to do this you will need to change the palette slider nudge settings in Quilt Options. While on the Quilt worktable, click QUILT > Options > Snap Settings. Under Nudge Settings, change the Palette slider increments to 1/32. You won't need this small increment for regular quilt blocks but for our 60° blocks it's very helpful.

IMPORTANT
If you print block, patterns, rotary cutting directions or templates for your 60° blocks, manually type in the size as opposed to using Size from Quilt.

Chapter 4: Drawing Outside the Box

Drawing a Seven Sisters Block

The little hexagonal stars in the *Seven Sisters* block share their background diamonds so it needs to be drawn on a *Base 5 grid*.

1. If you are beginning a new project file for this exercise, you will need **horizontal Base-5 grid (ED Isometric Grid_Base 5_Horiz)** to draw this block. If you saved the grid block previously in My Library, go there now and add the grid block to the Sketchbook. If you did not draw the horizontal Base-5 grid, you will need to do so now (see page 187).

2. Once you have added the grid block to your Sketchbook, retrieve it and place it on the worktable. Double-check that the settings on the Precision Bar are correct:
   - Block Width = **10.00**
   - Block Height = **8.66**
   - Snaps Horizontal = **20**
   - Snaps Vertical = **20**
   - Graph Paper visibility is turned **OFF**

3. Right-click and choose **Clear Guides** to remove any guides that might be currently visible. Then, **Select All (CTRL+A)**, right-click and choose **Convert to Guides**.

4. Using the **Line** tool, draw a full-size horizontal hexagon that fills the block. The tip and bottom are along the block outline.

5. In the upper-left of the hexagon, draw a six-point star, as illustrated. I find it easier to draw the crossed lines in the center first and then zigzag my way around these to draw the star points. Don't save this in the Sketchbook yet—our little star is still unattached!

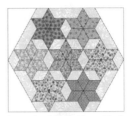

Example of *Seven Sisters* Block

Step 1

Step 2   off

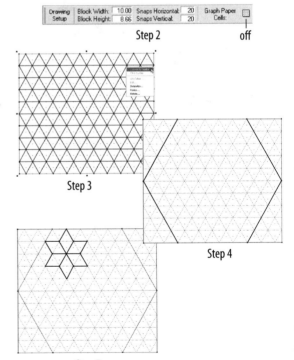

Step 3

Step 4

Step 5

192   EQ6 Pieced Drawing

Chapter 4: Drawing Outside the Box

Step 6
Pick

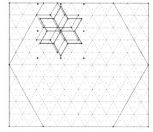

Step 6

Step 6

6 Switch to the **Pick** tool and click on the **small red square** to bring up the Symmetry box. Drag a marquee around the six-point star to select it (be sure you have all the lines of the star in your selection) and then **Clone** it. Move the clone over to the right so that it snaps into place, points touching the points of the first star.

7 While the second star is still selected, **Clone** it *five more times*, moving each successive star to its place. There are three rows of stars; two stars in the first row, three in the second and two in the bottom row. When you're done, click **Add to Sketchbook.**

What else can you draw on a Base-5 grid? How about a hexagon log cabin? Draw three logs skipping every other side, then draw logs between these. Work your way to the center until a small hexagon is formed. For a variation, draw a small hexagon star in the center.

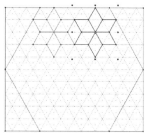

Step 6

Step 6

Step 7
Add to Sketchbook

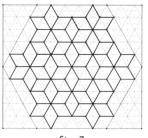

Step 7

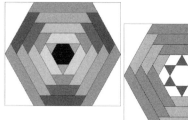

Variations of *Hexagon Log Cabin* Block

Companion Book Three   **193**

Drawing a Seven Sisters Block

Chapter 4: Drawing Outside the Box

Drawing 3-D Cubes

EasyDraw™ goes three-dimensional with the block you'll learn to make in this exercise. I'll give you some tips for coloring these blocks too—shading is the key to adding depth to these isometric cube blocks.

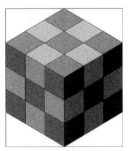

Example of *3-D* Block

1. If you are beginning a new project file for this exercise, you will need the *vertical Base-6 grid* (ED Isometric Grid_Base 6_Vert) to draw the blocks in this exercise. If you saved it previously in your My Library, go there now and add the grid block to the Sketchbook. If you did not draw the vertical Base-6 grid, you will need to do so now (see page 187).

2. Once you have added the grid block to your Sketchbook, retrieve it and place it on the worktable. Double-check that the settings on the Precision Bar are correct:

   - Block Width = **5.19**
   - Block Height = **6.00**
   - Snaps Horizontal = **24**
   - Snaps Vertical = **24**
   - Graph Paper visibility is turned **OFF**

3. Right-click and choose **Clear Guides** to remove any guides that might be currently visible. Then, **Select All (CTRL+A)**, right-click and choose **Convert to Guides**.

4. With the **Line** tool, draw a full-size vertical hexagon that fills the block. Left and right sides are along the block outline.

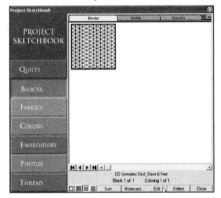

Step 1

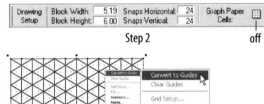

Step 2   off

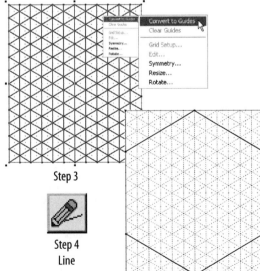

Step 3

Step 4
Line

Step 4

194 EQ6 Pieced Drawing

Chapter 4: Drawing Outside the Box

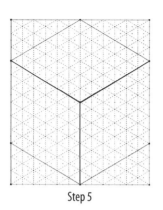

Step 5

Step 5
Add to Sketchbook

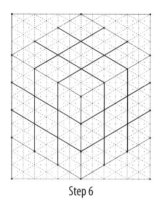

Step 6

Step 6
Add to Sketchbook

5 Draw three lines to the center dividing the hexagon in thirds and creating three diamonds. Click **Add to Sketchbook** to save your first cube.

6 Create a nine-patch cube. Draw two lines parallel to the sides of the diamond, spacing them every two guidelines apart in both directions dividing each diamond into a nine-patch. Click **Add to Sketchbook** to save your new nine-patch cube.

Draw some simple nine-patch pieced blocks in each of the diamonds. You can make them all the same or use three different ones. Look in the Block Library under Nine Patch and Nine Patch Stars if you need ideas. I drew an *Ohio Star*, a *Nine Patch Star* and a *Shoo Fly*.

3-D Coloring Tips
Take the time now to color your blocks. Try just using solid grayscale colors at first. For the basic cube you need only three values of gray: light, medium and dark. You get to decide where the light is coming from on your cube. I colored mine so that it looks like the light is coming from above the cube. For the nine-patch cubes, you'll need more shades or values. You add more shades and tints by right-clicking on any of the solid colors in the palette and choosing Add Shades and Tints.

When you are done playing with colors, try these other 3-D cubes.

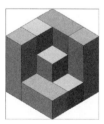
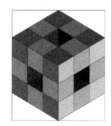
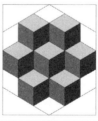

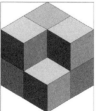

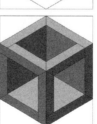
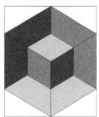

Variations of *3-D* Blocks

Tessellating 60's

An isometric grid is an excellent canvas for tessellating patches across a block. The trick is to make your block design repeat so that it also tessellates when set in a quilt layout.

Example of *Tessellating 60's* Block

1. If you are beginning a new project file for this exercise, you will need the *vertical Base-6 grid* (ED Isometric Grid_Base 6_Vert) to draw the blocks in this exercise. If you saved it previously in your My Library, go there now and add the grid block to the Sketchbook. If you did not draw the vertical Base-6 grid, you will need to do so now (see page 187).

2. Once you have added the grid block to your Sketchbook, retrieve it and place it on the worktable. Change the settings on the Precision Bar as follows:

   - Block Width = **12.00***
   - Block Height = **12.00***
   - Snaps Horizontal = **24**
   - Snaps Vertical = **24**
   - Graph Paper visibility is turned **OFF**

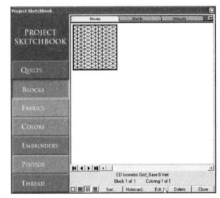

Step 1

Step 2   off

3. Right-click and choose **Clear Guides** to remove any guides that might be currently visible. Then, **Select All (CTRL+A)**, right-click and choose **Convert to Guides**.

*Note that we are working on a square block this time! Our isometric grid still works since it resizes to the block. Because our tessellating block will have lots of patches, we need to be absolutely sure that lines snap accurately along the right side of the block. Once the block is drawn it can be resized to hexagon proportions.

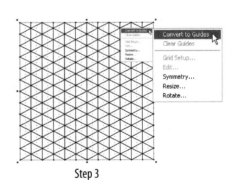

Step 3

Chapter 4: Drawing Outside the Box

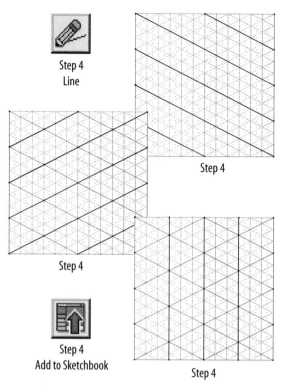

Step 4
Line

Step 4

Step 4

Step 4
Add to Sketchbook

Step 4

4   Click the **Line** tool. Begin by drawing a 3 x 3 diagonal grid on the block. Then draw three vertical lines dividing the diamonds in half. **Add to Sketchbook**.

5   In the first full triangle in the upper-right corner of the block, draw three radiating lines in the center. They should look like an upside down Y.

6   Switch to the **Pick** tool and click on the **small red square** to bring up the Symmetry box. Hold down the **SHIFT** key and select the three lines you just drew. Click **Clone** and move them to the next full triangle beneath the first one making sure that they snap into place.

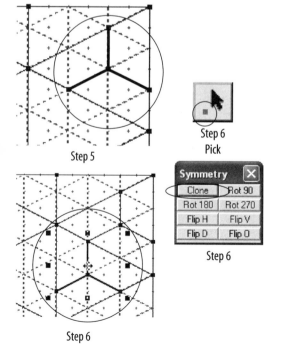

Step 5

Step 6
Pick

Step 6

Step 6

Tessallating 60's

Companion Book Three   **197**

Chapter 4: Drawing Outside the Box

7. *Repeat* **cloning** and **moving** until you have the three lines in all the full-size triangles. I find it easiest to work from top to bottom, one column at a time. You can **Add to Sketchbook** after each column is filled if you like.

8. To continue the repeat along the top of the block, follow the guidelines and draw zigzag lines in the half-triangles (that would be the bottom of our upside down Y). Then to continue the repeat along the bottom, draw short vertical lines on either side of the longer line of the half-triangles. **Add to Sketchbook** when you're done.

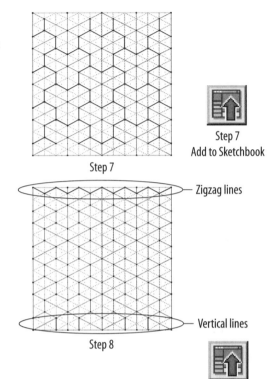

Step 7

Step 7 Add to Sketchbook

Zigzag lines

Step 8

Vertical lines

Step 8 Add to Sketchbook

Congratulations, you've just created a tessellating pattern! Remember to size the block in vertical hexagon proportions when you print the templates pattern or rotary cutting directions to keep the patches 60°.

The repeating design of tessellating trapezoids goes by several names, but most quilters today know it as *Inner City*. If you rotate it upside down, it's known as *Ecclesiastical*. Barbara Brackman's *Encyclopedia of Pieced Block* (also EQ BlockBase2) dates *Ecclesiastical* around 1882.

> **COLORING TIP**
> To make your *Inner City* (*Tessellating 60's*) block look three-dimensional, color two adjacent trapezoids in one of three different shades of gray or fabric value.

Here's another tessellating design you can try. I'm not sure of the name, but it looks similar to a block called *Whirligig*. Start with the 3 x 3 grid block saved in step 4. Draw upside down Y lines in one triangle and then draw right side up Y lines in the adjacent triangle.

You can also use this same Base-6 isometric grid to create unusual (and repeatable) 3-D designs like these three examples. Just follow the grid and let your imagination do the rest!

Example of *Whirligig* Block

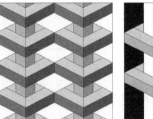

Variations of *3-D* Blocks

Chapter 4: Drawing Outside the Box

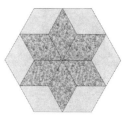

Example of *Hexagonal Pieced PatchDraw* Block

Step 1

Step 2

Step 3

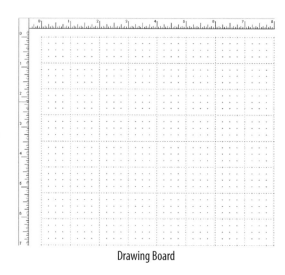

Drawing Board

Drawing Hexagonal Blocks with Pieced PatchDraw

I am always looking for ways to try new things in EQ6 and in the process I make all sorts of neat discoveries. In this exercise I get to share one with you! I discovered that we can make free floating hexagonal blocks on the Pieced Layer of PatchDraw (Pieced PatchDraw). It's so easy that the only reason it's here among the more advanced blocks is that we'll have to stretch the limits of EQ6 to do it. Are you with me?

> **Note**
> If you haven't worked through the exercises in Chapter 1 on drawing with Pieced PatchDraw, you will need to do so now. You will need to read through the Important Tips on page 18 as well as work through the exercise on drawing on the special Rectangle Grid on pages 23-24.

Create a Special Isometric Grid in Pieced PatchDraw

The first thing we'll do is create an isometric grid. Creating it is as easy as clicking and cloning!

1   Click **WORKTABLE > Work on Block**.

2   Click **BLOCK > New Block > PatchDraw Block**.

3   On the Precision Bar, enter these values pressing your keyboard TAB key after each:

   - Block Width = **8.00**
   - Block Height = **6.93**
   - Grid: **Rectangle**
   - Snaps Horizontal = **32**
   - Snaps Vertical = **32**
   - Graph Paper visibility is toggled **ON**
   - Cells Horizontal = **8**
   - Cells Vertical = **8**
   - The Auto fill patches option is turned **ON** (found under PatchDraw Options of the Drawing Board Setup)

Chapter 4: Drawing Outside the Box

4. Begin by drawing a 1" equilateral triangle in the upper-left corner. Using the **PolyLine** tool, begin at the corner on the block outline, **click** to the right 1" over, **click** at the center bottom of the division and then **double-click** back to the corner to close the patch.

> **Note**
> If you don't have the large grid dots showing on the drawing board, you may want to change that setting in the Drawing Board Setup options. Click BLOCK > Drawing Board Setup > Snap Grid. Select Display large grid dots.

5. With the patch still selected, click **Clone** and move it over 1" to the right in the next graph paper square. Click the **Pick** tool. Drag a marquee or use **CTRL+A** to select both triangles. **Clone** these and move them over to the next two divisions. **Clone** and **move** the selection two more times until you have eight triangles along the top.

6. Still using the **Pick** tool, drag a marquee around *seven* of the triangles, **Clone** and click the **Flip top and bottom** button. Move these so that they snap into place between triangles of the first row.

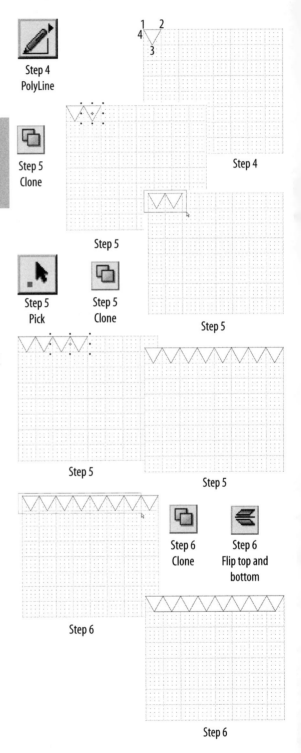

200   EQ6 Pieced Drawing

Chapter 4: Drawing Outside the Box

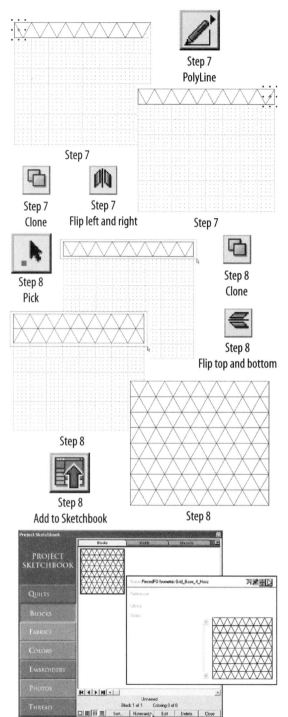

7. Switch back to the **PolyLine** tool. On the left end of your row of triangles, click and draw a half-triangle. **Clone** and click the **Flip left and right** button and move it to the other end of the row. That's all the drawing we need to do for this isometric grid!

8. Using the **Pick** tool again, drag a marquee around the entire row of triangles, or use **CTRL+A**. **Clone** and click the **Flip top and bottom** button. Move this new row down the block so that it snaps into place under the first row. Now select *both rows* using **CTRL+A** and **Clone** these *three more times* moving them into place until you have the block covered. **Add to Sketchbook.**

9. Take the time to name the block on its Notecard. Call this one ***PiecedPD Isometric Grid_Base 4_Horiz***. Click the "x" in the top-right corner of the Notecard window to close it. Once you have saved and named the block, continue to the next section and learn how to click and draw hexagonal blocks.

We now have a special isometric grid for Pieced PatchDraw! We've set the snap points at 32 x 32, so lines will snap at all intersections of our grid. It also shows us the center of the triangles.

Companion Book Three **201**

Chapter 4: Drawing Outside the Box

Building the Blocks

Let's start with a simple six-point star. The main difference in drawing it in Pieced PatchDraw is that we have to build the star with closed shapes. If you worked through the hexagon star section for EasyDraw™, you already know that most traditional hexagon blocks are made up of smaller hexagons, equilateral triangles, diamonds, trapezoids and a shape I call a *gem*. These shapes are easy to click and draw in Pieced PatchDraw. We cannot rotate 60° on the Rectangle grid of Pieced PatchDraw, but we can clone and flip! Now let's get started on that star…

10 Place the new PiecedPD Base-4 block on the worktable. **Select All (CTRL+A)**, right-click and choose **Convert to Guides**. *Turn off the graph paper visibility.*

11 Click on the **PolyLine** tool. The easiest way to build a hexagonal star is to first define the star shape. We'll begin by drawing the larger background diamonds first. Start at the top-center of the block (at 4") and click and draw a diamond on its side. It's two grid triangles tall and wide. You can draw around it clockwise or counter-clockwise. **Double-click** when you get back to the top center to close the patch.

12 **Clone** and **Flip left and right** and move it to the right of the first diamond so that the point touches point.

13 Switch to the **Pick** tool and select both diamonds, **Clone** and **Flip top and bottom**. Move these down to the bottom of the block.

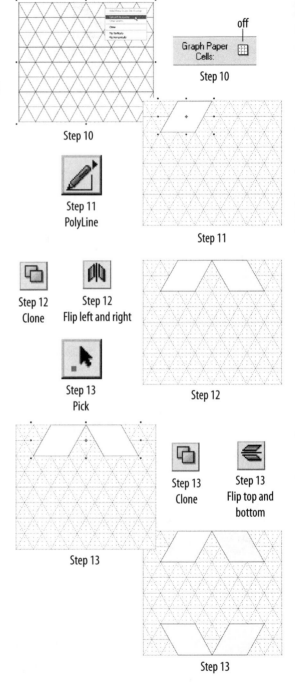

Hexagonal Blocks–Pieced PatchDraw

202 *EQ6 Pieced Drawing*

Chapter 4: Drawing Outside the Box

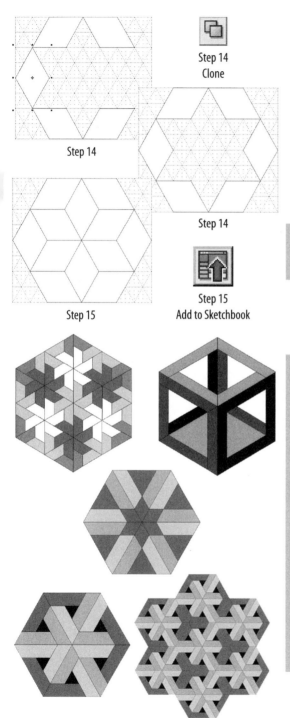

Step 14 Clone

Step 14

Step 14

Step 15

Step 15 Add to Sketchbook

Step 15

Variations of *Hexagonal Pieced PatchDraw* Blocks

14 Draw a vertical diamond (same size) on the left between the points of the horizontal diamonds. **Clone** this diamond and move it over to the right side of the block. You should now have a hexagon frame with with a blank star center.

15 To create the six-point star, you have a choice. You can click and draw the six diamonds in the center or you can clone the diamonds from frame—it's your choice! Do that now. You don't need to draw the patches outside the hexagon, leave those areas blank. When you have completed the center, click **Add to Sketchbook**.

> **Note**
> You can of course draw the patches for the background, but I'll leave that decision up to you!

Try several of the other stars from the previous section on Drawing Hexagonal Stars on page 188, or better yet, try creating new ones of your own. Here are some that I created in Pieced PatchDraw.

> **Notes**
> - If you want to try the cubes and 3-D designs create a new vertical Base-6 isometric grid in Pieced PatchDraw to use as guides for drawing the 60° patches. Block size and snap settings are the same as for the EasyDraw™ grid.
> - You can still print templates, foundation patterns and rotary cutting directions for these free-floating blocks as it does not include any part of the block you left blank.
> - *You need to know:* Sometimes when you view the hexagonal Pieced PatchDraw in the Sketchbook you will see ghost images of other blocks behind them. This does not affect the block nor does it happen all the time, but I thought I should warn you just in case you encounter it.

> **QUILT TIP**
> You can use this free floating hexagon block on Layer 1 of a Custom Set quilt layout or on Layer 2 like appliqué blocks. You can nudge your hexagons right up next to each other!

EQ6 PIECED DRAWING
Exercises in Pieced Block Design by Patti R. Anderson

Index

Index

Symbols

3-D Coloring Tips 195
3-D cubes 187
60° Blocks 182, 188, 192, 194, 199
7-10-7 Formula 158–160

A

Adding Blocks to My Library 12
Add Library 12
Anchor lines 131
Arc 80
Arc Grid 34, 37
Arc tool 79, 130, 132, 152
Aunt Eliza's Star 92, 96
Auto Fill 20, 138, 199

B

Basket 96
Basket blocks 65–75
Bear's Paw 58
Beggar's Block 56
Block Rulers 11
Block Size 58
Block Size when Drawing from Scratch 59
Block Size when Editing a Block 59

C

Centimeters 9
Change 80
Circle-based block in EasyDraw™ 157
Circle Grid 25, 32
Circle of Geese 122
Clear Guides 149, 188
Clone 22, 27, 35, 40, 83, 125, 169, 200
Color tab 137, 144
Compass-type blocks 29, 34
Compass to Foundation 118–121
Complex Foundation Block 136
Concord 46
Convert to Guides 94, 110, 148
Corner Block for Geese Curves 129
Create a repeating curve 126
Creating Isometric Guidelines 183
CTRL+A 13, 41, 110, 148
CTRL key 13
Curved Geese 126
Custom Block Library 12

D

Deleting Tracing Image 145
Dimension 1 and Dimension 2 43
Direction 80
Display large grid dots 19
Double Irish Chain 84
Drawing arcs 79
Drawing Board 56
Drawing Board Setup 99, 151
Drawing mode 20

Dresden Plate 110, 131
Drunkard's Path 79

E

Easy Draw™ Rule 62
Edit Arc box 106, 108, 111, 115, 123, 127, 128, 130, 152
Edit Line box 87
Eight-Bladed Pinwheels 165
Eight-Point Star 39, 157
Eight Point Star Grid 39, 44
Eight Slices of a Circle 157
Equilateral Triangle 182
Establish nodes 116, 140
Export Image 137

F

Fan Blocks 106
Fit image to block size 138
Flip left and right 41
Flip top and bottom 200
Floating hexagon block 203
Folded pinwheel 167
Foundation-Friendly Pattern 31, 42, 45, 50, 54
Foundation Pieced House Block 76
Foundation Piecing 42, 43, 78, 97, 108, 118, 129, 139, 142, 144
Four-Patch Drunkard's Path 81
Four Principles for Drawing Foundations 78

G

Garrett Windows Variation 22
Garret Windows 19
Giant Dahlia 37, 130
Going Crazy for Eights 175
Goose in the Pond 57
Grandmother's Puzzle 57
Grape Basket 68
Graph paper 21
Graph Paper Divisions 56, 60, 61
Grid dots 19
Grid tool 84–85, 86–87
Group 119
Guide Color 185

H

Half 115, 123, 128
Handle tent 127
Hexagonal block 183
Hexagonal log cabins 187
Hexagon star 186
Horizontal hexagons 187
House Block 76

I

Illusion of depth 153
Image tab 139
Import Image for Tracing 138

Index

Inches 9
Inner City 198
Inset Block 145
Isometric Grids for 60° Blocks 184, 185, 187, 199

K

Kaleidoscope 46
Kaleidoscope Grid 46, 49

L

LeMoyne Star 39, 157
Lightness 138
Line tool 61–62, 63
Log Cabin 58, 61

M

Mariner's Compass 114, 118
Marquee 21
Merge Blocks 156, 164, 174
Move a selected patch 18
Moving a group of selected patches 82
My Library 12

N

Name the block 185
New York Beauty 34
Nine-patch cube 195
Nine Patch Star 195

Node Select All 151–152
Notecard 22, 185, 201
Nudge Settings 190
Numbering tab 118

O

Octagon Grid 51, 53
Offset Shadow Block 148
Ohio Star 56, 195
On-point blocks 66
Open for Merging 164, 174
Options tab 119

P

Palette slider increments 190
Partition 106, 111, 115, 123, 128, 130
Perspective Frames 155
Perspective Window Frame Block 153
Pick tool 87, 94
Pieced PatchDraw 18
    Pieced PatchDraw Arc 34
    Pieced PatchDraw Circle 25
    Pieced PatchDraw Eight-Point Star 39
    Pieced PatchDraw Kaleidoscope 46
    Pieced PatchDraw Octagon 51
    Pieced PatchDraw Rectangle 19
Pinwheel in a Pinwheel 168
Playing with Merged Blocks 92
PNG 137

Index

PolyArc tool 25, 26, 34
Polydraw tool 19, 25, 34, 39, 46, 51
PolyLine tool 19, 39, 46, 51, 200
Prairie Braid Strips 97
Precision Bar 10
Pythagorean Theorem 158

R

Radiant Star 176
Rectangle Grid 19, 23
Repeater block 24
Resize 82, 145
Ring 25, 34
Rising Sun 171
Rolling Stone 161
Rotate 22, 27, 35, 40, 169, 178
Rot 90 83, 125, 169

S

Sampler quilt 190
Save Library 13
Sawtooth Star 57, 63, 72, 92, 96, 148
Seam lines 139
Sections tab 119
Selection box 21
Select All 110, 148
Select all 41
Select all nodes 151
Serendipity 92, 156, 164, 174

Seven Sisters 187
Shape tool 87, 106, 108, 111, 115, 123, 127, 128, 130, 140, 152
SHIFT key 13
Shoo Fly 145, 195
Sister's Choice 57
Six-point star 203
Sketchbook Full of Baskets 65
Snap Points 58
Snap to Drawing 11, 101
Snap to Grid 11, 18
Snap to grid points 56
Snap to Node 11
Spoke 25, 34
Square within a Square 58
Stagger 108, 111, 130
Stars 187
Sweet Gum Leaf 136
Symmetrical curve 127
Symmetry box 81, 169

T

Templates 121
Tessellating 60's 196
Tessellating Pinwheels 169
Tessellations 187
Thirds 127, 152
Tiled Square border 98
Tracing Images 136

Index

Transparent Blocks 150
Tree of Life 86
Triangles 187
Trims off the line extensions 141
True Hexagon 182
Twist and Turn 97

V

Vanishing point 154
Variable Star 63
Vertical hexagons 187
View Sketchbook 69
Virtual grid 56, 57

W

Wacky Blocks 101
    Wacky Churn Dash 103
    Wacky Five-Point Star 102
    Wacky Log Cabin 101
    Wacky Pineapple 102
    Wacky Pineapple Star 103
    Wacky Sawtooth Star 103
    Wacky Shoo Fly 103
    Wacky Star Cabin 103
Wedge 25, 34
What's that Grid 56
Wheel-type blocks 25
Wheel of Mystery 104
Whirligig Block 198
Winding Ways 104

X

Xings 87

Y

Y-seams 78

Z

Zoom In tool 99

About the Precision Bars

Each part of the Block worktable has a Precision Bar specific to the tab you are on, as well as the action you are making. The Precision Bar is available to make drawing and editing easier and more precise.

The Precision Bar is not turned on by default. To turn it on, click on the **VIEW** menu at the top of the screen, and choose **Precision Bar**.

For the most part, drawing blocks can be done without ever turning this feature on. The Precision Bar is to help make drawing more efficient for you. Many, if not all, of the features of the Precision Bar can also be found in the **Drawing Board Setup**, **Block** menu, and **Context** menus.

Drawing Setup	Block Width: 6.000	Snaps Horizontal: 24	Graph Paper Cells:	Horizontal 6	Snapping Options:				
	Block Height: 6.000	Snaps Vertical: 24		Vertical 6					
1		2	3	4	5	6	7	8	9

EasyDraw™ Block—EasyDraw™ Layer

The precision bar below stays the same for all tools on the **EasyDraw™** layer of the **EasyDraw Block** and **EasyDraw+PatchDraw** worktables.

1 **Block width and height:** Type a new size for your block into the boxes. To update the worktable to the new size, press the keyboard ENTER key or press the SPACEBAR. The block on the worktable will redraw to the new size.

2 **Number of snap points:** Type in the number of snap points you want.

3 **Hide/show graph paper:** Press the button down to turn on the graph paper lines. Press the button again to turn off the graph paper lines. These are just for visual reference. No snapping can be done to the graph paper lines.

4 **Number of graph paper cells:** Type in the number of cells horizontally and vertically you would like to see with the graph paper.

5 **Snap to grid points on worktable:** Press the button down to make your drawing points snap to the grid points of the worktable. Press the button again to turn snapping off.

6 **Snap to nodes of drawing:** Press the button down to make your drawing points snap to the nodes of a previously drawn segment. Press the button again to turn snapping off.

7 **Snap to lines and arcs of drawing:** Press the button down to make your drawing points snap to the lines and arcs of a previously drawn segment. Press the button again to turn snapping off.

8 **Hide/show image for tracing:** Press the button down to show an image for tracing. Press the button again to hide the image. (You must import an image for tracing before this will work.)

9 **More drawing board options:** Click the button to display the drawing board setup dialog.

Precision Bar Reference

            1   2   3   4   5 6 7 8 9 10 11 12

PatchDraw Block—Pieced Layer

1 **Block width and height:** Type a new size for your block into the boxes. To update the worktable to the new size, press the keyboard ENTER key or press the SPACEBAR. The block on the worktable will redraw to the new size.

2 **Grid style selector:** Click the down arrow to select a grid style.

3 **Number of snap points, Dimension, or Rings/Spokes:** Type in the number of snap points vertically and horizontally, snap points per polygon dimension, or rings and spokes you'd like for your grid. This section of the Precision Bar will change according to the grid that is selected.

4 **Hide/show graph paper:** Press the button down to turn on the graph paper lines. Press the button again to turn off the graph paper lines. These are just for visual reference. No snapping can be done to the graph paper lines.

5 **Number of graph paper cells:** Type in the number of cells horizontally and vertically you would like to see with the graph paper.

6 **Flip left and right:** Click the button to flip the selected patch left to right.

7 **Flip top and bottom:** Click the button to flip the selected patch from top to bottom.

8 **Convert selected segments to guides:** Click the button to convert the selected patch to a guide. A guide is for visual reference only. No snapping can be made to a guide.

9 **Clone selected segments:** Click the button to make a clone of the selected patch.

10 **Rotate selected segments:** Click the button to rotate the selected patch by a predetermined degree.

11 **Hide/show image for tracing:** Press the button down to show an image for tracing. Press the button again to hide the image. (You must import an image for tracing before this will work.)

12 **More drawing board options:** Click the button to display the drawing board setup dialog.

Tools Quick Reference

The Toolbars

Project Tools

 New

 Open

 Save

 Create Copy Project*

 Compress for E-mail*

 Print

 Export Selection*

 Export Image*

 Export Metafile of Block*

 Undo*

 Cut*

 Copy*

 Paste*

 Add to Sketchbook

 View Sketchbook

 Zoom In

 Zoom Out

 Refresh

 Fit to Worktable

 Watch a Video

 Display Dynamic Help

 Work on Block

 Work on Quilt

 Customize Toolbars

> *These tools are not on the toolbar by default. To add them to the toolbar, click the Customize Toolbars button > click Add/Remove Buttons > click to put a check next to the tools you want to add. Click away from the list to close it. (To restore the default tools at any time, click Customize Toolbars > Restore Default Tools.)

Companion Book Three   **213**

Tools Quick Reference

The Toolbars

Quilt Tools

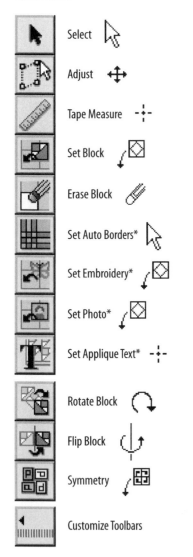

Color Tools (Quilt worktable)

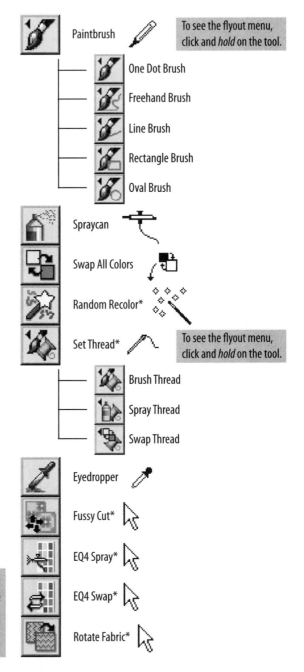

*These tools are not on the toolbar by default. To add them to the toolbar, click the Customize Toolbars button > click Add/Remove Buttons > click to put a check next to the tools you want to add. Click away from the list to close it. (To restore the default tools at any time, click Customize Toolbars > Restore Default Tools.)

Tools Quick Reference

The Toolbars

EasyDraw™ Tools

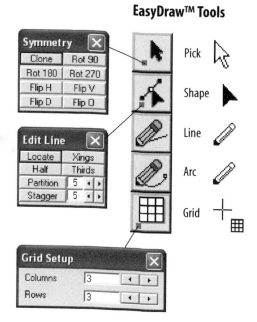

Tracing Tools

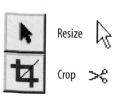

Color Tools (Block worktable)

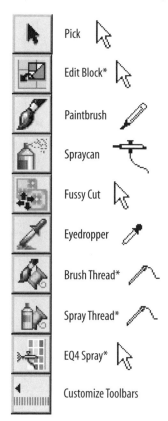

> *These tools are not on the toolbar by default. To add them to the toolbar, click the Customize Toolbars button > click Add/Remove Buttons > click to put a check next to the tools you want to add. Click away from the list to close it. (To restore the default tools at any time, click Customize Toolbars > Restore Default Tools.)

Companion Book Three

Tools Quick Reference

The Toolbars

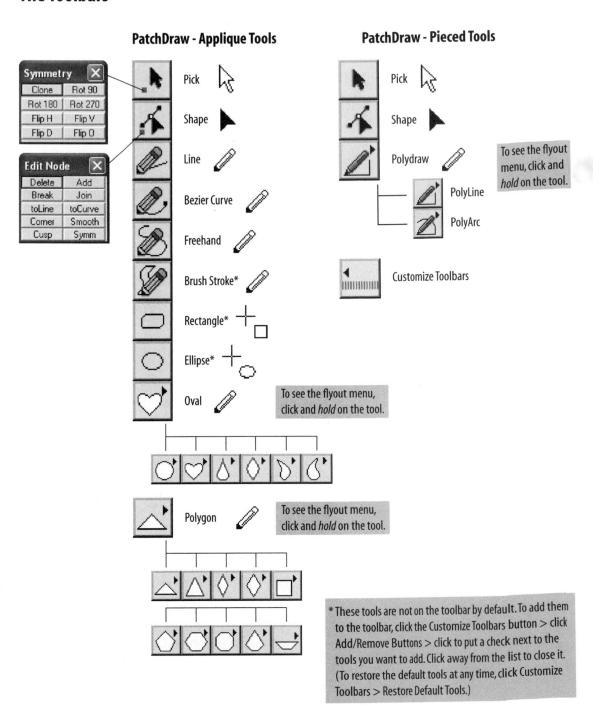